IN DREAMS WE MOOR

IN DREAMS WE MOOR

ROBERT C. MARWICK

BRINNOVEN

ISBN 1 899851 04 6

British Library Cataloguing in Publication Data.
A catalogue record for this book is available from the British Library

Cover design by Siân Braes
Cover photograph © Willi Murray

Typesetting and origination by Brinnoven, Livingston
Printed and bound in Great Britain by Redwood Books, Trowbridge

CONTENTS

Acknowledgements

I wish to thank the following persons who kindly provided the photographs used in this book: Cathleen Craigie, Edith Gibson, Tom Gibson, Muriel Johnston, Olive Kemp, Bill and Freda Murray, Willi Murray, Edna Penny and John Vetterlein.

I am indebted to Duncan Robertson for permission to reproduce the poem, 'Sons of the Isles', written by his grandfather, Duncan J. Robertson, and also to Alison Fraser, Archivist at the Orkney Library, for her valuable assistance on numerous occasions during the preparation of this book.

Robert C. Marwick
Kilwinning
January 2000

Sons of the Isles

There is a spell woven by restless seas,
A secret charm that haunts our Island air,
Holding our hearts and following everywhere
The wandering children of the Orcades;
And still when sleep the prisoned spirit frees,
What dim, void wastes, what strange, dark seas we dare,
Till, where the dear green Isles shine low and fair,
We moor in dreams beside familiar quays.

Sons of the Isles! though ye may roam afar,
Still on your lips the salt sea-spray is stinging,
Still in your hearts the winds of youth are singing;
Though in heavens grown familiar to your eyes
The Southern Cross is gleaming, for old skies
Your hearts are fain, and for the Northern Star.

D.J. Robertson
1860–1941

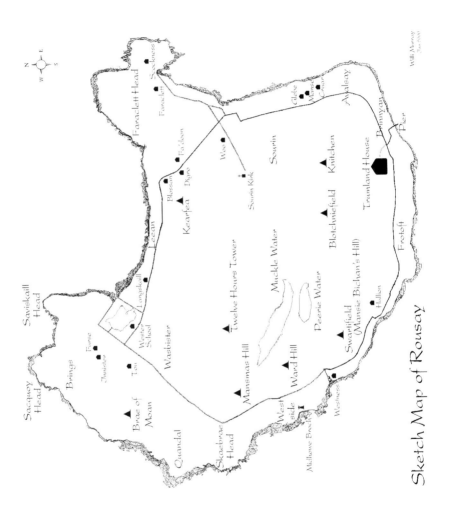

Sketch Map of Rousay

Willi Murray Jan 2000

Letter to an Australian Cousin

Dear Pat,

In my previous letters to you I wrote mainly about our mutual Marwick ancestry from the island of Rousay, in Orkney, but have not so far told you much about the island itself and the way of life there. When your great-great-grandfather left Rousay nearly 150 years ago most of the islanders made their living from farming and fishing. That has not changed over the years, although the methods employed in these industries have undergone tremendous changes. The most marked changes in the way of life have taken place in my lifetime and it is on that period that I shall concentrate in telling you about the island, although I shall frequently touch on earlier times as well.

I have to tell you at the outset that I believe, as many others do, that there is something especially appealing about islands. Some people seem to regard islands as places of romance which have been cast adrift from the neighbouring land mass to become little kingdoms in a dreamworld of their own, havens of peace and tranquility, away from the throb and bustle of life in the cruel world of reality. Viewed from a distant shore on a summer's day, islands can so easily beguile the innocent into believing that what they are seeing across the water hints at the promise of Paradise.

Very few of the islanders that I know would describe their island as a paradise but a conversation with them would soon reveal that, in many cases, their relationship with their island goes a long way beyond mere liking or familiarity. Some of them may have been born and brought up on the island, while others may just have lived there for a time or be frequent visitors but what they have in common is a bond that has developed between them and their island, a bond that may not easily be broken.

As someone born and brought up on an island. I feel that strong ties bind me to the place of my birth. As I grew up I came to regard these ties as restrictions to be cast aside as I reached out towards the wider world beyond my island's shores. Such is the folly of youth. What I did not realise at that age was that Rousay had already put its mark upon me in my early years and would always claim me as one of its own. In time, I began to be aware of this as I kept being drawn back to its shores by a longing that would not be denied and by bonds of affection and affinity which, as I eventually came to acknowledge, I had no desire to cast off.

If I am away from home and someone asks me where I come from I will reply with the name of the place where I now live. However, if the question is put in the form, 'Where do you belong?' then I feel that I must give a very different answer because there is only one place to which I feel that I truly belong, and that place is Orkney. This is a claim that my birthplace has put upon me. I am a captive, a willing captive.

Apart from frequent holidays, I have not lived in Orkney since my early twenties and of course absence has made the heart grow fonder. With that admission made I invite you to come with me as I journey around Rousay looking at the island as it is now and sometimes wandering down memory lane to see it as it was in the past. On the way, some light might be cast upon the nature of the bonds that exist between islanders and their islands.

Yours aye,

Robert

THE BRINIAN

Orkney lay under Norse rule from the ninth century until 1486 when the islands were ceded to Scotland. Consequently, almost all place names are of Norse origin. In his book, *The Place-names of Rousay,* Dr Hugh Marwick traces the name Rousay back through its various forms to Hrolfsey, Hrolf (Rolf) being a common personal name among the ancient Norsemen. Later forms of the name were Rollesay in the late fourteenth century, Rolsay in the fifteenth century, Rowsay in the early sixteenth century, with the present form first appearing in 1549.

After Hoy, Rousay is the hilliest of the Orkney islands. Its highest hill is Blotchnifield which reaches 816 feet and two others, Kearfea and Knitchen, rise to over 750 feet. To those with the energy to climb their gentle slopes they afford splendid views over the North Isles and parts of the Mainland, the largest of the Orkney islands. Apart from the Mainland, Rousay is the only Orkney island that has a road running round it. The road is 14 miles long and throughout its length is never more than a few hundred yards from the coast. At many points the road rises to several hundred feet above sea level, opening up excellent views of the surrounding countryside and coastline as well as across the sea to neighbouring islands. Most of the arable land lies between this road and the shore.

Rousay is divided into three main districts, Wasbister, Sourin, and Frotoft with a much smaller one known as the Brinian squeezed in between the latter two. The Westside, now uninhabited, lies between Wasbister and Frotoft. It is in the Brinian that a visitor to the island will land after a half-hour trip on the ferry *Eynhallow* across from Tingwall on the Mainland.

The *Eynhallow.* (*Photograph by Bill Murray.*)

The ferry, a modern development of the wartime landing craft, drives itself on to a concrete slipway on to which the bow door is then lowered to form a ramp. The *Eynhallow* is not a drive-through vessel such as those that serve the more outlying islands so vehicles have to reverse on to it, a task calling for a degree of skill and precision some drivers do not profess. For them, a member of the crew will obligingly drive the car on board. One Rousay farmer would have spurned such assistance had it been offered as he reversed his car down the slipway. After all, had he not reversed his tractor and trailer aboard on many occasions in recent months? In his mirror he mistakenly took one side of the bow door for the other and would have ended up in the water had he not responded just in time to the frantic shouts of the crew members. When he eventually got aboard and emerged from his car he staggered about pretending to be drunk. As he explained, 'I did not want folk to think I could be that stupid when I was sober.'

The Rousay slipway lies between a breakwater on one side and the old pier on the other. The pier had catered for the steamer service from Kirkwall for over 100 years before the present roll-on roll-off ferry service began in 1987. The steamer called only once a week. Because there was not always sufficient water at the pier the sailing times varied from week to week according to the state

The *Shalder,* pictured here at the Tingwall pier in 1984, was the last motor-boat to serve on the Tingwall–Rousay ferry service. It was operated by Mansie Flaws of Wyre. (*Photograph by Willi Murray.*)

of the tide. Although not built as a vehicle ferry the steamer could carry a very small number of vehicles at considerable cost and no less inconvenience as almost everything had to be hoisted on or off the ship. The service offered by the steamer was very inferior to that now provided by the ferry which makes five or six return trips daily to Tingwall at much lower fares than those on the steamer.

Latterly very few passengers travelled on the steamer as an efficient motor-boat service operated by Mansie Flaws of Wyre was in operation conveying passengers to Tingwall where a bus bound for the county town of Kirkwall would meet them. In the summer months the boat back to Tingwall on a Sunday evening was always crowded with those returning from a weekend or day visit. On one such occasion the sea was like a millpond and everyone was enjoying the crossing and the beauty of their surroundings. A musician who happened to be on board produced his fiddle and began to play to entertain his fellow passengers. Reels and strathspeys and slow airs floated across the water adding to the enjoyment of all on board, many of whom were tourists. The crowning touch came when a school of seals, attracted by the music, appeared on the scene and swam alongside until the fiddle had to be put away as the boat approached the Tingwall jetty.

The cluster of buildings that has grown up near the pier is the nearest that Rousay has to a village. Until recently, there had always been a grocery shop at the pier and one or two others elsewhere in the island. With the coming of the ferry many islanders now motor into one of the Kirkwall supermarkets to buy their groceries, leaving only enough business to keep one shop open on the island.

In my childhood the shop at the pier belonged to Willie Marwick. He had a horse-drawn van which he took around the island once a week. Willie always seemed to want to move faster than the horse's measured pace, giving the impression that he was dragging the animal along rather than leading it.

Shortly after the war Willie bought a car so that he could run a taxi service. One day a farmer who had shipped some cattle hired Willie to drive him home from the pier. A few days earlier Willie had had the misfortune to capsize his boat while out sailing. This gave the farmer an irresistible opportunity to have a little fun at Willie's expense and as he climbed into the car he said to Willie that he hoped he was better at driving a car than he was at sailing a boat. These were the last words he was to utter until he had been set down at his farm on the other side of the island after the most hair-raising car journey he had ever endured. Never again, he vowed to himself, never again. Willie had scared the wits out of him with a display of devil-may-care driving at a breakneck speed that had broken every rule in the Highway Code. As his passenger staggered from the car Willie smiled to himself and drove off at his usual sedate pace.

Standing cheek by jowl with Willie Marwick's grocery shop were Charlie Logie's joiner shop and the adjoining smithy of William Sutherland. The joiner and the blacksmith were great friends but this did not stand in the way of either one having some fun at the other's expense whenever the opportunity arose. One day Charlie happened to look out of his window and spotted the minister, with a determined look on his face, heading in his direction. Charlie suddenly

Charlie Logie. (*Photograph courtesy of Tommy Gibson.*)

remembered that, six weeks earlier, he had promised the minister that he would attend right away to the repair of some broken windows at the manse. He had no excuses to offer the minister so he slipped out the back way and into the smithy next door. He quickly explained his predicament to his friend and asked if there was anywhere he could hide till the coast was clear. The blacksmith suggested that Charlie could climb into the rafters where the minister was unlikely to spot him in the poor light. Charlie followed the suggested course of action and was crouched on a rafter like a hen on its perch when the minister entered the smithy.

'I'm looking for Mr Logie', he announced, 'but he's not in his workshop. Do you happen to know where I might find him?'

'Oh, yes', replied the blacksmith cheerily, 'he's sitting up there in the rafters.'

The smiddy at the pier closed down many years ago as did the other two which I remember operating in the island when I was a boy. The shoeing of the large Clydesdale horses from the farms formed a major part of the blacksmith's work and this disappeared almost overnight with the rapid introduction of tractors after the Second World War. Prompted either by nostalgia or a sense of loyalty to the breed, some farmers in Orkney still keep one or two of these majestic animals which attract a great many admiring looks whenever they appear in public. In the South teams of Clydesdales are kept by some brewery firms for show purposes and can sometimes be seen pulling brightly painted drays along city streets presenting a magnificent spectacle too seldom seen nowadays.

The road from the pier climbs up for a little way before it joins the main road which circles the island. Turning to the right, we soon come to a roadside cottage called Cubbie Roo. A cubbie was a large, round, straw basket carried on the back by a shoulder strap. Modern versions of the cubbie serve as laundry baskets or as fireside storage for logs or peats. Cubbie Roo is believed to be a local form of Kolbein Hruga, the name of a Norse chieftain who had a castle on the nearby island of Wyre. The story that has come down through the ages in Rousay has it that Cubbie Roo was a giant who planned to build a bridge between Rousay and Wyre. In preparation for this task, he was carrying stones in a cubbie when the shoulder strap broke and the stones fell out to form a heap or a roo, to use the local term. The cottage was named after this pile of stones which closer examination was later to reveal was an ancient chambered burial cairn which had collapsed in upon itself.

Another old story about Cubbie Roo places him on the island of Westray, some miles to the north, from where he flung a huge rock at an enemy giant on Kearfea Hill in Rousay. It fell rather short of its mark and now lies near the shore in the Leean in Wasbister. It is known as the Finger Steen. Those who look for them will still find on the rock the imprints of the giant's fingers.

Down at the shore below Cubbie Roo there is a ruined kirk surrounded by a graveyard. Between it and the pier are several houses each of which has a piece of ground stretching down to the shore. In bygone days the people of Wyre used to cut peats in Rousay and piled them up along this stretch of shore prior to boating them across the Sound.

The introduction of the ro-ro service in 1987 has brought an enormous increase in the amount of vehicular traffic to and from Rousay. Scenes like this at the Rousay pier are not at all uncommon during the summer months. (*Photograph by Bill Murray.*)

Rousay used to have three kirks all of which were well attended. Two of them have been closed for many years. Close by the ruined kirk stands another which was in regular use until very recently. Now it is in need of costly repairs which cannot be afforded by the small congregation and is up for sale. Rousay no longer has a resident minister so part of the manse now serves as the church with a minister coming periodically from the Mainland to conduct services and to carry out pastoral duties.

SOURIN

After leaving the Brinian the road turns north around the side of Knitchen Hill before dipping down into a small valley which is drained by the Burn of Cruar. Perhaps I should explain, Pat, that a burn is our Scots term for a stream, what you in Australia would call a creek. The small croft after which the burn is named is situated down near the shore. The occupant of Cruar I remember best was Mrs Alexina Craigie, a delightful old lady who lived to the age of 102. Before her marriage she had worked as a maid in Trumland House, the home of General Burroughs who owned most of the island at that time. The General was a harsh and vindictive landlord and latterly very few people in Rousay had a good word to say of him. Despite this, Alexina remained strongly loyal to her former employer till the end of her days, refusing to listen to anyone speaking ill of him. One day, towards the end of her life, she and a neighbour were discussing the General. The neighbour, who was aware of Alexina's tenacious loyalty, mischievously remarked that the General had died in a public toilet in London. Alexina was horrified. Pulling herself up to her full height, she declared, 'General Burroughs was never in a public toilet in his life!'

On another occasion Alexina and a friend were discussing Craigie families in Rousay. Alexina was doubly proud of her Craigie name having borne it before her marriage as well as after. 'Some people complain', she said, 'that we Craigies consider ourselves better than other folk.' Then, looking her friend straight in the eye, she added, 'But we are!'

Beyond the Burn of Cruar stands the minister's manse surrounded by the fields of the Glebe farm. This farm, which still belongs to the Church, has been let out to a succession of tenant farmers for the

Alexina Craigie. (*Photograph courtesy Cathleen Craigie.*)

past 100 years but prior to that it was farmed by the minister himself. One of his farmhands 150 years ago was a young man called Simpson Skethaway who hailed from the nearby island of Stronsay. After a few years Simpson and another young man, John Gibson, who was one of my great-great-grandfathers, married sisters from the neighbouring farm of Knarston, and before long were joint tenants of that farm. Each tenant had his own stock but the labour and everything else invested in the farm were shared equally as were all the crops at the end of harvest. At first sight, such an arrangement would seem to be fraught with difficulties and bound to give rise to frequent disputes. There must have been a large measure of goodwill and friendship that overcame any difficulties encountered for the arrangement outlived both Skethaway and Gibson and continued under their heirs well into the twentieth century.

A Royal Commission, headed by Lord Napier, was set up by the government in 1883 to look at the condition of crofting and crofters in the Highlands and Islands of Scotland. When the Commission sat at Kirkwall a great many complaints came from crofters in Rousay where the laird, General Burroughs, had been operating a harsh policy of steadily increasing rents. Among the complainants were Skethaway and Gibson. Burroughs argued that their farm, Knarston, with an acreage of nearly 80 acres was too large to qualify for consideration as

The Manse and Glebe, in Sourin, looking towards Egilsey. (*Photograph by John Vetterlein.*)

a croft. The tenants maintained that it should not be looked at as one farm but as two crofts. They were asked if they paid the rent jointly or separately. They replied that they paid separately and that they had receipts to prove it. However, the receipts were in Rousay and it became clear to them that a decision in their favour would depend on production of these documents. That night Simpson Skethaway, who was then 60 years of age, rowed out to Rousay, procured the receipts, and rowed back to Kirkwall, a round trip of 28 miles. When the Commission met in the morning for its final sitting the co-tenants produced the documents and won a decision in their favour. That decision later earned them a welcome reduction in rent.

Pat, your great-great-grandfather, Thomas Marwick, would have known John Gibson very well as his wife, Ann Gibson, was John's sister. Thomas's farm at Woo lay only about half a mile from John's at Knarston. He would not have known at first hand of the tussle with the laird as that occurred some years after he emigrated.

Above the road, about half a mile beyond Knarston there used to be a small thatch-roofed croft house called Midgar. In the early 1920s it came by inheritance into the possession of Alexander Marwick who had been born and raised there. He lived in Glasgow where he seemed to have acquired some wealth, part of which he had invested in the purchase of a number of farms in Sourin district. In Rousay he was known as 'The Duke' because of the airs and graces he adopted whenever he appeared in the island. He had the old cottage at Midgar demolished and a large two-storey house erected in its place. He had plans for imposing entrance gates and a driveway leading up to the house but a shortage of funds came in the way of completion.

About that time a boat he owned was mysteriously destroyed by fire at the shore below Midgar and a story circulated in Rousay to the effect that this was part of an insurance fraud in which The Duke was involved. Shortly afterwards, the farms he owned were sold off and The Duke was seldom seen in the island again. No one seems to have known how he acquired his wealth or how he lost it. The house he built at Midgar was never occupied except on a few brief holiday occasions. A later owner removed the roof to be used elsewhere and most of the walls were demolished at the same time. One wonders what nickname The Duke would have been given had he lived later in the twentieth century. 'The Chancer' comes to mind.

A few hundred yards further along the road the major part of the district of Sourin comes into view. Facing us are the farms which lie stretched out along the southern slopes of Kearfea. Old Thomas Marwick's farm of Woo lies in the centre of the district. The old single storey house which he left in 1862 is still standing but in a ruinous state. A new dwellinghouse was built about the turn of the twentieth century and the old house was converted for use as a shed and cattle shelter.

From the Muckle Water up in the hills at the other side of the island the Suso Burn winds its way past the Sourin peat banks and down through the valley till it reaches the sea in Egilsay Sound. Near its mouth stands the meal mill which, in the 200 years of its working life, was powered by the water coming down the burn. This was the biggest by far of three mills that operated in Rousay at one time, the others being at Saviskaill in Wasbister and Hullion in Frotoft. When the two smaller mills closed down, the Sourin mill, in addition to coping with all the grinding required in Rousay, also ground grain boated over from neighbouring islands.

When I was a boy every house in the island had its supplies of oatmeal and bere meal which in various forms were a staple and important part of the islanders' diet. Bere is a form of barley. The main bread on the table was bere bannock and as children we were not allowed any white bread, or loaf as we called it, until we had eaten the required amount of bere bread that we considered less palatable, but which, in hindsight, was probably much better for us. Porridge made from freshly ground and deliciously malty tasting oatmeal was not a breakfast dish in our house. We always had it for supper. Small quantities of bere are still grown in Orkney and both bere meal and bere bannocks can be bought in some shops.

In 1984 two Rousay fishermen, brothers Hugh and Bruce Mainland, sold their boat and used the proceeds and their savings to start up an industry which was new to the island. It was fish farming, and in particular, salmon farming. Having been advised that Rousay waters were not sheltered enough for fish cages, they built onshore tanks at Frotoft through which seawater could be pumped. The brothers financed this first step in the development of the business from their own resources and with the aid of grants from the Highlands and Islands Development Board and Orkney Islands Council.

In the early years of the project salmon fetched a much higher price on the market than it does now and the brothers' efforts were rewarded with high profits which were ploughed back to expand the business. At first they bought in their supplies of smolt, about one and a half years on from being hatched, for onward rearing but this arrangement soon began to stand in the way of further expansion when hatcheries could not meet their increasing orders for young stock. It was then that they decided to set up their own hatchery financed by profits of earlier years and further injections of public money from time to time. In 1986 the hatchery was established in Sourin where the Suso burn, backed up by the Muckle Water, could provide all the water that it would need. They knew from personal experience that the water quality was suitable as it supported an enviable number of trout which they had fished for when they were boys. They obtained permission to use the burn water and eventually bought the nearby mealmill along with which came complete control over the burn and the Muckle Water.

A winter's day in Sourin. (*Photograph by John Vetterlein.*)

They had been warned by their technical advisers to expect losses of 50 per cent in their hatchery stock so they were greatly encouraged when their first year's losses fell far short of that figure. After three years the hatchery was not only meeting their own needs for breeding stock but was also supplying other farms in Orkney as well as some further afield. By 1987 the tanks at Frotoft could no longer contain the farm's increasing stock and large cages had been constructed and positioned in fairly sheltered water at Sourin.

In the early days of the farm the shop price of salmon was £6–£7 per pound, but it is now less than £1. As the price fell the Mainlands had to sharpen up their working practices and become more efficient in order to compete. At first they had done all the processing, packing, and marketing of their own product but later all the fish farmers in Orkney came to the conclusion that it would be mutually advantageous to get together in a co-operative venture to handle this side of their businesses. Eventually the Mainlands came to control this marketing company. The Rousay farm, with its annual output of 500 tons contributes about 25 per cent of the marketing company's total.

In 1990 the Mainlands embarked on experiments on behalf of the industry to find out how halibut could be farmed. After six years and numerous setbacks they considered that they were within four or five years of overcoming most of the obstacles that stood in the way of this species being farmed as successfully as salmon. They were confident that halibut would be extensively farmed within ten years, and that attention would then turn to other species especially those whose numbers in the wild are declining through over-fishing. However, the loss of revenue resulting from the temporary closure of the hatchery left insufficient funds for the halibut project and it has now been placed on hold meantime.

Recently the whole enterprise suffered a severe setback when an escape of fuel oil polluted the burn water on which the hatchery depends. The entire stock of the hatchery consisting of a million young fish perished or had to be destroyed. They were left without any fish to put into the cages for two seasons. As their cages and hatchery were disease free they could not risk bringing in young stock from elsewhere. A pipeline had to be laid to draw unpolluted water from further upstream before the hatchery could get back into operation.

Through their enterprise the Mainland brothers, in the course of a few years, have built up from scratch a business in Orkney with an annual turnover of £2.5 million, giving much needed employment to 14 people in Rousay.

Down at the shore, near the mealmill stands the house of Lopness which was the home of Stanley Gibson when I was a boy. Stanley was a stonemason and there are many examples of his work in the island that bear witness to his craftsmanship. Almost all the buildings in Rousay are built of stone. Unlike you Australians, Orkney farmers have to winter most of their stock indoors and consequently there are more buildings on our farms than there are on yours. Fortunately, good building stone was in plentiful supply as can be seen from the numerous small quarries found all over the island, and consequently no one had far to go to find stone for a new house or byre or other building. With every district having three or four stonemasons in the old days, there were more of them than of any other trade. Despite the plentiful supply of building stone in Rousay, most buildings erected nowadays are built of concrete blocks which are cheaper because of the cost of quarrying stone.

A few hundred yards along the road from Lopness can be seen the ruins of the house known as Guidal, the birthplace of Rousay's most distinguished son. He was Dr Hugh Marwick who for many years was Director of Education for Orkney. He was a noted scholar and writer.

The ground rises more gradually on the south side of the Suso burn. At one time about a dozen families lived here on small crofts created out of poor hilly land but in the past 60 years all the crofts have been vacated apart from the three which lie nearest to the main road. All the tiny fields of these small crofts now lie untilled, given over to rough pasture for the animals of a larger neighbouring farm. There are many old empty crofts like these on the island. Almost all are on sour, unproductive, hilly ground with rough, wet, and muddy access from the road.

Here in the centre of Sourin stands the island school which was built in 1960 to replace the old district school on the same site as well as the schools in Wasbister and Frotoft. It is classed as a Community School by virtue of the fact that the building serves both as a school and a community centre. In addition to the classrooms and the hall, the school has two rooms set aside for the use of community organisations but which are available for school use at other times. I have written elsewhere* about the history of schooling in Rousay and therefore will not spend time on it here.

Wedding receptions in Rousay are held in the school as it has the only hall in the island. Until about 1930 a wedding in Rousay usually took place in the barn at the home of the bride. A meal would be provided in relays in the house for all the guests. If the wedding took place in the summer time the younger people would pair off and, preceded by a fiddler or a piper, would set out for a walk with the bridal party at the head of the column. In Wasbister, the walk went around the loch, a distance approaching two miles. By the time they had returned, the older guests would have finished their meal and the walkers then sat down to theirs. The celebrations usually went on all night and the weary dancers would wend their way home as breakfast time approached. Farm weddings went out of favour as church weddings became more popular, but the reception was still held at the bride's home after the church ceremony. Before long it became the common practice to have the wedding in the church

---

*From *My Rousay Schoolbag*, Brinnoven, Livingston (1995).

and the reception in the local hall. Couples who preferred a simpler wedding could be married by the minister in his manse or could choose to have a civil ceremony in Kirkwall.

Recently it has become possible for civil marriages to take place in Rousay. The local registrar of births, marriages, and deaths is now authorised to conduct such ceremonies which apparently have to take place in Council owned premises. In Rousay the school is the only place deemed suitable and this arrangement is probably doubly suitable as far as the registrar is concerned as she is one of the teachers. After leaving her classroom at the end of a school day she may well find herself returning a few hours later to conduct a marriage ceremony.

Across the road from the school, the electric power company has located a sub-station which, I have no doubt, is an essential installation if the island is to have an efficient power supply but it is a dreadful eyesore for all that. How on earth was planning permission given to site this structure in this particular location where it is completely out of keeping with its surroundings? It is like having a pig sty in a flower garden; it offends not only the eye but every other sense that tells us what is fitting. Surely it could have been located in a less conspicuous place nearby where its ugly starkness would not have smacked the onlooker in the eye in the way it does here, right beside the road. By their very nature such structures are not usually aesthetically attractive but their starkness and harsh outlines can be disguised to a considerable extent by painting them in colours designed to blend in as far as possible with those of the surroundings. Surely something of that kind could be tried here.

Next door to the school is the former Co-op shop and store. All through my childhood the Co-op van was a familiar sight on the road as it did its twice a week circuit of the island. At first it was pulled by two horses but in the 1930s a lorry was acquired and the van body was carried on that. The van carried not only groceries and a selection of small household goods but also numerous two-gallon cans of paraffin stacked in racks on the outside. Everyone needed paraffin for oil lamps in those days when no one entertained thoughts of mains electricity ever reaching the island. At that time the old wick lamp with its flame protected by a glass funnel was beginning to give way to the much brighter Tilley lamp which burned vaporised oil within a delicate, gauze mantle. One minute the vanman might be measuring out a gallon of paraffin for a customer and the next handing her an unwrapped loaf of bread. Hygiene was not something that was of great concern to the vanman. He probably had never heard of the word but it is likely that neither had some of his customers. When I recall the lack of hygiene in the handling of food in those days it makes me wonder how any of us survived.

On its rounds the van collected large quantities of eggs which the farmers' wives brought along to exchange for their groceries. Before the lorry appeared on the scene the conveyance of eggs had become an increasing problem because near the end of the Saturday round, late at night, the van had to ascend the very steep Leean road, a tough task for the horses at the end of a long day.

The first vanman I remember was Sammy Inkster who was a very small man. Although having the misfortune to be slightly hunchbacked he appeared to us children to be very strong as he heaved large bags of poultry feedstuff about with apparent ease. It amused us that every heave was accompanied by a very audible, and probably involuntary, 'Humph!'

Sammy had a mile or two to travel to work so he acquired a motorbike. One day when it came time for him to go home for dinner he started the machine, let the clutch in and tried without success to move off. He revved the engine a bit more but still the machine would not move. This was because, unknown to Sammy, two of the bigger boys from the school had sneaked up behind him and had lifted the rear wheel just clear of the ground. Then, as Sammy revved the engine even harder, they let go and the machine, with Sammy holding on for dear life, shot off like a bullet from a gun. As with many of the practical jokes perpetrated in those days, it is unlikely that the possibly dire consequences of this one had been given much thought.

It is only a short way from the Co-op down to the shore at the mouth of the Suso burn. It was there that we used to gather whelks on our way home from school at the time of the low Spring tides. We would dump our schoolbooks in the roadside ditch with a flat stone on top of them and make our way down to the shore to fill our bags with whelks which we took home to be boiled. A hairpin was a very useful tool with which to unwind them from their shells once they were cooked. I can still recall how very tasty they were but I do not think I would care to eat them now. Next morning we would recover our books from the ditch, thankful that there had been no overnight rain. Soaking wet books would have been difficult to explain away had we been caught. Considering that our schoolbags stank to high heaven for weeks afterwards, it is surprising that explanations were never called for by the teacher.

Another tasty bite was provided for us by courtesy of any farmer who happened to have a field of turnips growing beside the road. By early autumn the turnips were the size of tennis balls and at their sweetest and most succulent. After it had been pulled from the ground, the turnip had its shaws twisted off and its taproot broken off on a stone or a fencing post. It could then be easily peeled to become a tasty after-school snack for a hungry child.

The road running east from the crossroads in the middle of Sourin takes us towards the farms of Faraclett and its neighbour, Scockness, occupying its own peninsula. Pat, Scockness is the earliest traceable home of our Marwick forebears. They took over the farm in 1783 and were evicted about 40 years later because of a dispute with the laird over kelp-making. Kelp was the ash produced by burning certain kinds of seaweed in stone lined pits at the shore. Twenty tons of wet seaweed yielded about a ton of kelp. The ash fused into a solid mass which had to be broken up before being shipped south to chemical plants. The main chemicals obtained from kelp were potassium sulphate (about 12 per cent) and iodine (about 4 per cent). In the 1830s cheaper sources of these chemicals were found elsewhere and the kelp market, on which Orkney was heavily dependent at that time, collapsed. Farming, operating at little more than subsistence level, supported by fishing, could not provide a living for Rousay's population of about 1000 without the ready cash that came from kelp. Large numbers emigrated to Australia, New Zealand, Canada, and the USA, countries which were then looking for settlers for their vast expanses of land. (Subsidised packages were available in some cases and the new settlers were given an allocation of land at little or no cost in some countries.) The exodus from Rousay that began at that time has gone on ever since but may recently have been halted.

Looking towards the Holm of Scockness, with Cruar in the forground. (*Photograph by John Vetterlein.*)

The Head of Faraclett is a large expanse of moorland teeming with birdlife. Rousay, like the rest of Orkney, supports large numbers of birds, particularly sea-birds. Most islanders can identify all the birds most often seen and many derive considerable enjoyment from studying them. A glance at the Orkney Tourist Board's brochure reveals that the wealth of birdlife is one of the main attractions put before prospective visitors. Despite having been surrounded by a great variety of birds during my childhood, and despite hearing others able to identify dunters and divers, starlings and sparrows, blackbirds and bonxies, terns and teeos, snipe and skarfies, it surprises me that I managed to remain in almost total ignorance about all things birdy. I know that seagulls are large white birds which follow fishing boats and ploughmen and will eat almost anything. I know too that sparrows are cheeky little birds that hop around the garden stealing the nuts my wife puts out for the blue-tits but that is about as far as my knowledge goes. I sometimes feel slightly ashamed of this and resolve to take more interest but this resolve soon fades and disappears. While I admit a lack of interest in the subject I must also admit that I feel rather envious of those who can derive so much pleasure from studying birdlife.

In many parts of Orkney can be seen standing stones, long slabs of rock stuck upright in the ground. Some of them are in groups, the best known of which is the Ring of Brodgar in the parish of Stenness on the Mainland. It originally had about 60 stones of which 27 still remain standing, many to a height of ten feet or more. Rousay has some standing stones though none as tall as those at Brodgar. One of them stands on the land of Faraclett. It is called the Yetnasteen, a name derived from Old Norse meaning 'stone of the giants'. It is a large slab of rock about three feet wide and ten inches thick standing about seven feet high. One cannot but wonder why and how these huge slabs of rock were put in place in many parts of the Orkney landscape. Vast numbers of people must have been marshalled to move and erect them. It is easy to envisage these monoliths, especially if seen in the last rays of the evening light, as silent sentinels standing guard over the surrounding countryside, and it is little wonder that, in some people's minds, they came to be invested with unusual powers.

It is said that in the early hours of every New Year's Day the Yetnasteen takes two giant steps down to the nearby loch for a drink. There are even those who claim to have witnessed this but somehow their accounts of the event always seem to lack the clarity necessary for them to be credited with any significant measure of accuracy. Something to do with the time of year, I am told.

A story is told of a party that was held at the farmhouse of Faraclett a long time ago. It was an important social occasion for all those who were invited. For those left off the invitation list it was a welcome opportunity to work some mischief. The centrepiece of the supper-table was to be a steaming hot plum-duff, not just any ordinary run-of-the-mill plum-duff, but one made in a cloth, that delicious Scottish sweetmeat known as a clootie dumpling. The mix had been put on to boil in mid-afternoon, not in the farmhouse kitchen where the five-hour cooking time would have raised too much steam, but in an outhouse. As suppertime approached the lady of the house and one of her daughters went out to bring in their masterpiece. They suspected that all was not well when they found the door of the outhouse, which they had earlier left securely snecked, standing ajar. Imagine their horror when they saw that the huge pot was off the fire, with the lid lying on the floor, and the clootie dumpling gone.

It was a lovely, moonlit night and a group of young men sat around a large stone down at the nearby shore. On the stone lay a cloth to which clung a few crumbs, all that remained of the clootie dumpling from Faraclett. That afternoon one of the group had noticed the smoke from the chimney of the outhouse and had guessed what was going on there. As darkness fell it had been an easy task to alert his friends and to make the necessary arrangements for their delicious moonlit supper down at the seaside.

My sister-in-law, Evelyn, is an expert at making a clootie dumpling. The ingredients are not measured out with any degree of accuracy. It is just a handful of this, a pinch of that, and a spoon or two of the next, yet the end result is always a culinary delight. Many years ago I was at a wedding in Rousay at which we were served great slabs of cold clootie dumpling at four o'clock in the morning. Seldom have I tasted anything that has matched that in sheer deliciousness. It was one of Evelyn's best.

It was out in this part of Sourin that Mary Ann lived. She was very fond of her pet Shetland pony and was heart-broken when it died. She asked her husband to bury it and by the following day it had disappeared from the scene. However, he had not gone to the trouble of digging a grave but had instead thrown the dead animal into the sea confident that that would be the last he would see of it. Unfortunately the tides were not running in his favour and a day or two later the carcase was washed up on the shore not far from where it had been consigned to the deep. It was found there by two youths who recognised it as Mary Ann's pride and joy. That night they dragged it up the short distance to her house and propped it up, stiff-legged with rigor mortis, against the haystack with a wisp of hay in its mouth. Next morning, Mary Ann looked out from the kitchen window and saw her old pet helping itself to its breakfast from the haystack. She threw up her hands in delight and exclaimed, 'Oh my, thoo bonie thing, thoo're come back!'

If we return to the crossroads and continue westwards a short walk takes us up to the old Sourin Kirk. It was built as the result of a momentous upheaval in the Scottish Church in 1843 when hundreds of ministers and their congregations left the Established Church and set up the Free Church of Scotland. This event, known as the Disruption, affected all parts of Scotland. Among the ministers who left, taking most of his congregation with him, was Revd George Ritchie of the Established Kirk in the Brinian. That was the beginning of the Free Kirk in Rousay.

Kearfea, with the Sourin Kirk in the foreground. (*Photograph by John Vetterlein.*)

I claim a tenuous connection with George Ritchie through my great-grandmother having been a servant girl at his manse in Sourin prior to her marriage. She named her fourth son, my grandfather, after her former employer and ever since, the name George Ritchie Marwick has appeared in every generation of our family, but only in the Canadian branch.

Ritchie was a man of great drive and was well thought of by his people. Within two years of the Disruption he and his followers had acquired the funding to build their kirk in Sourin as well as the Free Kirk school in Wasbister. This kirk became part of the Church of Scotland at the re-union that took place in 1929.

Pat, your ancestor, Thomas Marwick of Woo was an elder in the Rousay Free Kirk and the Kirk Session minutes of May 1862 record a glowing tribute to him on the occasion of his departure for overseas.

As a boy I lived in Sourin for a time and was dragged along to the Kirk every Sunday. The service was followed by a Sunday School which was taken by one of the elders, John Inkster of Woo. In our bible lesson one Sunday, the use of a flail was mentioned. Some of us may have known what a flail was but none had seen one so John took us down to his barn nearby where he had an old flail which he demonstrated in use for our benefit. I suppose there must have been other things that I learnt at Sunday School but how a flail was used is the one that most readily comes to mind.

A hundred years earlier the young James Leonard from the small croft of Digro on the side of Kearfea Hill would have attended this same Sunday School. He grew to manhood in Ritchie's time and went on to become the precentor and choirmaster, and also an elder, a man who could be described as a pillar of the kirk. He saw the laird's grip on the lives of the crofters becoming tighter as he demanded ever increasing rents which were beyond their ability to pay and fast becoming beyond their endurance to bear. The opposition to this harsh regime was centred in the Free Kirk in Sourin with James Leonard emerging as the chief spokesman for the crofters as the time approached for the visit to Orkney of the Napier Commission. The story of the struggle that ensued is vividly told by William P.L. Thomson in his book *The Little General and the Rousay Crofters*. Of Leonard's ability and character Thomson says:

> Burroughs was to find him an implacable opponent, a powerful and able man, not to be cowed into submission as most crofters could be. Although he might waver under pressure from the laird, he was ultimately determined to defend his principles even when this led to eviction and having to leave the island.

At the Commission hearings in Kirkwall, Burroughs, unlike other lairds, declined to give an undertaking not to take retaliatory action against tenants who spoke out against him. Despite this warning of what the consequences were likely to be, Leonard told the Commission of the plight of the Rousay crofters. Burroughs retaliated by evicting Leonard from Digro. This led to his leaving Rousay because he was unable to find accommodation for his large family in the small part of the island outwith Burroughs' control. This vindictive action by the laird was considered particularly harsh coming at a time not long after the Leonards had lost three of their children in a diphtheria epidemic. Eventually this distressed family settled in Oban where Leonard obtained employment in the coal trade. At a later stage he became a merchant in that trade and appears to have prospered to the extent of owning the first car in Oban.

In his conclusion, Thomson writes:

> Of those involved in Rousay's troubled years, no one emerges with more credit than the stern, unbending James Leonard and no one was called upon to make greater sacrifices. He never returned to Orkney.

The Sourin kirk was no longer needed for Church use after the mid-1960s. It was abandoned and allowed to fall into disrepair. Wind and rain and countless birds have reduced the place to its present sorry state. Surely some more dignified, yet inexpensive, means such as fire could have been employed to end the useful life of this building. This rotting heap is a shameful memorial to the courage of men like George Ritchie and James Leonard and is no credit to those in the kirk responsible for it. James Leonard, in particular, was a man whose name Rousay people should speak with pride. For his brave stand against oppression, and for the high price he had to pay in defence of his principles, James Leonard ought to be commemorated in the island of his birth. It is good to learn that moves are now under way for a fitting memorial to him to be erected near his former home at Digro.

Not far up from the crossroads we come to the island's only shop, at Essaquoy. Chris and Marion Clark who own it came to Rousay from the South Pacific in 1983 and started growing vegetables and fruit on Essaquoy's few wind-blown acres. They soon found that their crops required shelter and so polythene tunnels were erected and all their produce is now grown in them. Transporting vegetables from the island ran away with any profit made and consequently all their efforts now go into growing and marketing strawberries. Most of their crop is sold within Orkney but some of it finds its way further afield with Sweden being their most distant market so far.

From the crossroads the main road climbs in a straight line up the lower slopes of Kearfea until it levels out as it rounds the shoulder of the hill, at a height of 465 feet, before it sweeps down across the steep slopes of the Leean into Wasbister. At its highest point, reputedly the highest of any road in Orkney, stands the little crofthouse called The Blossom. The name deteriorated into its present form from Blossan, a feature on the nearby hill. In my young days this house was known as Hammermugly, a name with a fine ring to it. What a pity it is that several other houses in the island have also been given 'flowery' names such as Ivybank and Briarlea, not to mention the Brinian triplets, Ivy, Rose, and Daisy, all of whom have cottages named after them. Why adopt such insipid, prissy-sounding names, alien to the islands, when the hills and coastline of Rousay offer a wide choice of otherwise little -used names of Norse origin that have a robust and familiar ring to them? Hammermugly, Noustigar, and Longatong, for instance, are names that roll off the Orcadian tongue with an ease born out of centuries of familiarity.

Downhill from Hammermugly and tucked in under the brae, almost out of sight from the road, stands Fa'doon. Its name is obviously derived from its situation. A short descent over the brae brings into view the dwelling house and numerous outhouses, all with their flagstone roofs intact. Every year the owner of this croft, Jeemie Grieve, spends an extended summer here in the house where he was born 90 years ago. During this annual visit necessary repairs and maintenance are carried out to keep the property in good order. When I visited Jeemie last year his 14-year-old great-grandson was spending a holiday with him. As we climbed back up to the road the lad drew my attention to a small house he had built into the face of the brae. It was just big enough for him to crawl into but he had fitted it with such refinements as a hinged door and a glazed window. Its flat flagstone roof was covered with squares of turf neatly peeled from the grassy brae.

Seeing this little house and the obvious pleasure the builder had derived from constructing it took me back to my childhood when I saw numerous little structures, similar to this one, which had been built by teenage boys. Some were built in corners where two existing walls reduced the amount of building required, and others were to be found in some of the island's numerous quarries where the young builders did not have far to carry the stones they needed. If built in a convenient location, a small building of this kind could come in useful as a ducky hoose or a chicken pen.

As I left the lad of Fa'doon he asked if another book listing the names of all the houses in the island would ever be published. 'If it ever is', he added, 'I would like this house to be in it.'

'What name have you given it?' I asked.

'Tripup', came the answer.

'An unusual name', I remarked. 'What made you think of it?'

'Well, you see,' he explained, 'I had many a trip up this brae to carry all the stones up here.'

This lad's little house, like his great-grandfather's, is aptly named.

Descending another terrace or two from Fa'doon we come to the bottom of the valley lying between Kearfea and the Head of Faraclett. Here lies the old farm of Swandale, the land of which now belongs to a large neighbouring farm, leaving the house and steading unoccupied and falling into ruin. Sinclairs farmed this place for a long time, Archie being one of the first of them.

A great deal of illicit brewing went on in Orkney in his time and Excisemen were constantly on the prowl trying to track down those engaged in it. A quantity of malt ready for brewing was all the evidence they needed. One day Archie saw an Exciseman coming down over the braes towards the house. He immediately ran to the barn, heaved a sack on to his back and made for the nearby shore as quickly as he could. The Exciseman, seeing this as a blatant attempt to get rid of evidence, gave chase. He soon gained ground on his quarry who seemed to be making very slow progress even allowing for his load and the strong head wind blowing in from the shore. When the gap had closed to a few yards Archie turned and emptied out the contents of his sack, relying on the wind to do the rest. The irate Exciseman realised he had been duped when he found himself covered in a thick layer of corn chaff with aans (or bristles) that cling to clothing with an infuriating persistence and which are equally irritating to the skin. What added to the Exciseman's anger and, no doubt, to Archie's enjoyment of the situation, was the knowledge that the ploy had been a mere diversion to give those back at the farmhouse time to find a secure hiding place for the malt.

The Sinclairs of Swandale, who are numbered among my ancestors, were reputed to be very mean, with every penny that came their way being made a prisoner. It is said that Archie would go about in rags rather than spend money to make himself look more respectable. A story is told of a visitor to Swandale finding Archie, dressed in his drawers, busily working away as usual. He had removed his trousers to avoid unnecessary wear and tear on them while he carried out some work in the farmyard midden.

From Hammermugly we get a splendid view over the North Isles. With a large part of Sourin in the foreground the view stretches across the Sound to Egilsay with Eday beyond it. Sanday and Stronsay lie to the east and Westray to the north with Noup Head, its northern extremity, jutting out to the northwest. This must be one of the finest views to be obtained on any public road in Orkney and for 5000 years people must have climbed up to this spot to admire the beauty of the scene laid out before them on a warm, sunny day. Islands and green holms lie low in a sparkling sea beneath the canopy of a

Sourin, from the summit of Kearfea, looking towards Egilsey. The radio equipment sitting on and around the triangulation point was being used to gather data for a study into the movement of seals around the islands. (*Photograph by Willi Murray.*)

friendly sky. There is warmth in the sun despite the breeze that is never far away in Orkney, and we hear the cries of the birds made anxious by our presence. All the elements of sea and sky, land and nature combine to form a scene pleasing to all our senses. Over the centuries of human habitation on this island many people must have gazed out over this scene and, for a time, had their thoughts turned away from their daily cares.

The friendly beam from the lighthouse on Noup Head used to be a welcome companion for me on the many occasions I travelled the lonely Leean road between Wasbister and Sourin when I was a boy. There were other lighthouses around the North Isles to keep me company on a dark night but Noup Head was the best one, because it was near enough and bright enough to frighten away the bokkies, those spectres of the night which, as all children know, lurk in the shadows just beyond the fringes of vision. And then, there were also the dreaded marauding otters that were said to frequent the Leean. Had I not heard that if one of them grabbed a leg in its powerful jaws it did not let go till it heard the bones crunch? Thankfully, the friendly Noup Head light kept them all at bay, and I walked the road unscathed.

The cliffs at Faraclett Head. (*Photograph by John Vetterlein.*)

I remember one summer evening, some years ago, I was travelling up the Leean road in a car. We had almost reached the top when I asked the driver to stop. I got out and looked at Faraclett Head as if I had never seen it before. The evening sun was shining directly into the face of the cliffs, and although I had looked on that scene hundreds of times in years past I had never before realised how remarkable it was. How many public roads, I wondered, could offer me such a striking view of spectacular cliff scenery at such close quarters? It had taken an absence of a few years to open my eyes for the first time to the grandeur of that scene which had been part of my daily surroundings for a large part of my early life.

Half way down the Leean, near a slight dip in the road, there is a spring which fills a small hollow in the roadside banking with crystal clear water. In the past this spring was said to be known to every horse in Wasbister and, without being told, they would stop there to refresh themselves after covering the steepest part of the long climb up the hill. How refreshing is the hard, cold, clear water from a natural spring such as this compared with the soft, brackish, chemically treated rainwater many of us get from our taps.

A little farther on is a roadside quarry that was still in use when I was a boy. Here the roadmen toiled, quarrying the stones which they then broke down by hand into road metal, the pieces being about the size of a golf ball. After many months of back-breaking work they might end up with a flat-topped pile of material 50 or more feet long by 10 feet wide and 3 feet high. Similar piles of road mettle could be seen at other quarries around the island.

At that time, major road repairs were carried out at two- or three-year intervals. A steam-powered road roller was shipped out to the island. Along with it came a large wooden caravan in which the roller driver, Geordie Carter, and his assistant lived during their stay in the island. Local farmers were hired to cart the road metal to the sections of road to be repaired. After it had been evenly spread it was covered with a layer of crushed clay. This material was readily obtainable in many parts of the island. Next came the water cart which had been filled at the nearest burn or dam. It sprayed its load over the clay to give it a good soaking. Rolling then began and was continued till the metal was well bedded in with the clay. If this work was going on near the school we all crowded round watching the operation with great interest. The road roller, that steaming, snorting monster, grabbed and held our attention as it moved up and down crunching the stones beneath its mighty wheels. Up in the cab stood Geordie, his face blackened by soot and oil but smiling through it all. He could always find time to have a cheery word with us as we eagerly gathered round whenever he brought the roller to a halt. We boys used to marvel at the exciting life Geordie had, driving that giant of a machine all day and getting to live in a caravan into the bargain. I am sure that we all envied him.

When all the repairs had been completed in one area, the caravan, on its iron wheels and with the water cart attached to its rear, was hitched to the roller and with Geordie Carter at the controls the whole cavalcade would trundle noisily away in clouds of smoke and steam, bound for its next destination.

On roads where there was little motor traffic and nothing moving fast this type of surface lasted for a long time. Sixty years ago there were no more than half a dozen cars in Rousay. The first car I remember belonged to the local doctor. I remember it well because it was the first one I ever rode in. In the 1950s and 1960s there were still so few vehicles in the island that any seen on the road could be instantly identified. By that time nearly every house had a telephone and if the postboat was spotted approaching the island with a policeman on board word of it would have reached every house by the time he set foot ashore. Rousay folk are very considerate in matters of this kind. They know that policemen have to come to the island occasionally in connection with sheep dipping and similar routine matters but they see no reason why they should spoil the visit by burdening them with extra work. So never an unlicenced or uninsured vehicle will the lawmen find on the road. This allows them time to enjoy a cup of tea and a scone in the restaurant while waiting for the next ferry back to Tingwall. Such handy things, these telephones. Oh my, yes.

Here in Britain a motor vehicle has to undergo an annual roadworthiness test once it is three years old. In Rousay the need for this test is waived as the island has no authorised testing centre. Another concession allowed is that a learner driver does not have to be accompanied by a qualified driver. With access to the island being now both easy and comparatively cheap, Rousay's roads are having to carry an ever increasing volume of traffic. This reaches its peak in the summer months as more and more tourists venture off the Mainland with their cars to explore the other islands which the modern ferries have brought within their reach. Some bus tour companies now include Rousay in their choice of tours. Tour buses from as far afield as Germany have been seen on the island, prompting one wag to comment, 'I wonder what they thought of the Westside autobahn.'

Tourism has recently overtaken agriculture as Orkney's biggest industry in terms of earnings. Every year increasing numbers of tourists pour into the county, drawn by the many attractions the islands have to offer. Rousay, with its scenic beauty, its abundance of prehistoric sites of interest, and its wealth of wildlife, seems bound to attract even more of these visitors in the future than it does at present. Most islanders are happy to share these attractions with visitors but rightly complain about the few thoughtless tourists who leave open gates which allow stock to wander and about those who pay scant heed to other people's privacy. It is good to see that in some parts of the island, particularly at Faraclett Head and along the Westness shore, signposts have been erected to indicate the paths tourists should follow. Stiles and kissing gates have been provided to give easy access through fences, thus avoiding any need for tourists to open stock gates. It is to be hoped that more of this will be done for the benefit of both farmers and tourists. It is a much better way of dealing with wandering tourists than the appearance of a sign at the roadside giving the blunt warning, PRIVATE – NO TOURISTS.

Many of the tourists are day visitors some of whom bring their own transport while others come prepared to do a bit of hiking or to join a minibus tour of the island. A complaint sometimes heard is that the island's economy gains little or nothing from these day visitors as they spend no money while they are on the island. Many of those travelling in organised parties even bring packed lunches with them. The small hotel in Frotoft, the restaurant at the pier, and the minibus operator are the most obvious beneficiaries of any money that is spent, with the island shop gaining a significant amount of passing trade as well. These businesses benefit from the tourist trade only because they have set out to do so.

Tourists to Rousay, like tourists everywhere, have money to spend but Rousay offers them very little on which to spend it. More spending by day visitors will not happen until services, facilities, attractions, and goods are on offer to encourage such spending. Wasbister, for example, being the part of the island which lies furthest from the pier, could well accommodate some tourist facility of the kind that would encourage visitors to spend money. If tourists arrive in ever increasing numbers as predicted it will surely be much more sensible to make reasonable provision for them to be given organised access to places of interest, and for the islanders to devise means of deriving some economic benefit from their visit, than to bemoan their presence in a futile attempt to hold back the tide. It is for the people of Rousay to seize the opportunities provided by tourism in order to enhance the economic health of the island. It makes more economic sense to cash in on tourism than to continue complaining about it as if it were an imposition upon the island.

WASBISTER

L ocally, the district of Wasbister is known as Wester. Most of it is exposed to view as we descend the Leean road which sweeps down across the long north face of Kearfea overlooking the Bay of Saviskaill. The district is saucer shaped with one side of the saucer tipped towards the sea. It is drained by several fast-flowing burns into the Loch of Saviskaill in the middle. There are two islets in this loch which, with many other sites in the island, provide us with evidence of the various peoples who have gone before us on these islands. One, called Burrian, is undoubtedly artificial, and of the type that originated as a crannog. The other, Brettaness, on the eastern shore is more often a peninsula than an island nowadays. In 1984/5 it was excavated by local archaeologist who found it to be artificial, built up in layers of occupation over a long period on a gently sloping promontory of bedrock. Burrian has not been excavated but both sites may have been in use over roughly the same time span. How far back into prehistory their origin lies is not yet clear, but Brettaness was certainly occupied in the Iron Age and Pictish period, with some use extending into the Norse era. Remains were uncovered of Pictish buildings and a substantial structure from the Iron Age similar to a small broch (a defended round house) remains unexplored. Further insight into life here during the later Iron Age Pictish period should be provided by the good preservation of animal bone and other environmental evidence on the site.

Most of the land in the low-lying parts of Wester is rich and productive, but stretched out along the hillside on the south side of the district lie 15 or 16 small crofts, all except two of which have long since been abandoned. What bare harvests that sour soil must have

Wasbister, from the Brae of Moan, (*Photograph by Willi Murray.*)

yielded up for those who struggled to survive on it. In particularly hard times they survived only through the charity of kindly neighbours who might not have had much themselves but nevertheless were willing to share it with those who had even less.

At the foot of the Leean road we come to the farmhouse of Langskaill, one of the island's largest farms. Two hundred years ago Langskaill was farmed by David Gibson who was one of my more interesting ancestors. A distinguished descendant of his, Dr Hugh Marwick, said of David that in his youth he had had an 'adventure' with a woman from Burness, a little croft up on the hill above Langskaill, as a result of which twins had been born. David went on to marry three times, his third wife being a widow who was also an ancestor of mine. I can therefore claim that David married two of my great-great-great grandmothers. He fathered ten children and had 46 grandchildren. Within three or four generations his progeny formed a considerable part of the island's population.

Long ago, travel within an Orkney island, and between neighbouring islands, was much more difficult and therefore less frequent than it is nowadays. Consequently, marriage partners were sought from within the island, often from within the same district. A degree of inbreeding in the population resulted from this but down through the

Wasbister, from the abandoned crofts above Cogar, looking towards Westray. (*Photograph by John Vetterlein.*)

generations there was an awareness of the problems that could arise. Marriage between first cousins was frowned upon and discouraged especially if the families concerned were aware of some weakness on one or both sides. However, this atmosphere of disapproval of such marriages did not prevent some from taking place but the arrival of new blood in the island from time to time prevented any serious problems arising.

In by-gone days when social events such as dances were few and far between, young couples had to find other ways of meeting if their courting was to make any progress. A common practice was for the young man to try to sneak into the girl's bedroom after everyone in the household had gone to bed and the parents had been given sufficient time to get off to sleep. If access could not be gained by a window he would remove his boots and enter as quietly as he could by the door. In country districts doors were never locked.

The story is told of a father who heard noises coming from his daughter's room, and got up to investigate. He found the son of a well-to-do local farmer in bed with his daughter. As the surprised young man sprang out of bed and grabbed his clothes the father pacified him, saying, 'Jeust lie still, Hughie beuy. Jeust lie still.'

A similar story from long ago concerns a couple caught red-handed by the girl's father. He simply closed the door upon them and returned to bed. He had noted, however, that the young man in bed with his daughter was someone who had not long before inherited £100 from an uncle.

'Wis there somebody in there?' asked his wife, anxiously.

'Yaas.'

'Did thoo pit him oot?'

'Na, na, I let him be. Hid's no every night there's a hunder pound in the hoose!'

The road levels out just beyond Langskaill and continues past the school which stands close to the loch. This school, one of three in the island at that time, was the first one I attended. We did not get many visitors who might divert us from our work but one who came every year was Dr Bannerman, the Medical Officer of Health, to carry out medical checks on five- and nine-year-olds. On one such visit he sent a note home to a boy's parents advising them that their son's vision was defective and that he needed glasses. On the next steamer day the father went into Kirkwall and bought him a pair. Not for that lad a carefully conducted vision test with lenses being prescribed which would match his needs.

Dr Bannerman was a person who never seemed to smile. His boorish, brusque manner frightened children and we dreaded being examined by him. I do not remember my first school medical but I do remember the preparations for it. This involved having our heights and weights recorded. Measuring our heights was no problem for the teacher but ascertaining our weights was because there was no set of scales in the school. The problem was solved by sending us along to a neighbouring farm to be weighed on the scales that were normally used for weighing sacks of potatoes.

One of the results of the relative isolation of life on an island at that time was that most people reached adulthood without ever having been exposed to such common childhood ailments as chickenpox, measles, or mumps. One summer, when I was about 14, I came down with mumps a few days after arriving home from school in Kirkwall for the long summer holidays. This caused consternation in the island. No one could remember when there had last been a case of mumps in Rousay so there was little or no immunity to it in the inhabitants. Their

Saviskaill Bay. (*Photograph by Willi Murray.*)

dread was natural as these ailments tend to give adults a much harder time of it than they give children. Some others in the family caught the infection from me with the result that we were all ostracised by the rest of the community for most of that summer, well past the period of any risk of further infection taking place. During this period an older brother who was home on holiday, and who had had mumps some years earlier, went to a dance in Sourin and was none too pleased at being asked to leave.

Looking back on them now, I must have found the five years I spent at this little school a carefree and happy time although I cannot recall ever feeling full of the joys about being there. Presumably, I made reasonable progress as I have no memory of encountering any difficulties in my schoolwork except on one occasion. There were three in my class, the other two being girls. After a time I began to notice that I invariably got more sums right than they did and no doubt felt a little smug about it. On one occasion, after a few days' absence, I returned to school to find that the girls had been taught long multiplication during my absence. The teacher took me aside and quickly explained the process before setting the three of us to work on some examples. Marking time came and with it the horror of finding that all my answers were wrong while the girls had scored full marks. After a little more instruction I began to get the hang of long multiplication and made sure that there was no repeat of that day's dreadful state of affairs.

There were times at school that could be described as joyous. One of them that came around every year began when preparations for the Christmas concert and party got under way. With only about twenty pupils on the roll, each of us had to appear in several items on the programme. I remember some preparations being made for an item which involved more than half our number but which never reached the final programme. I remember it clearly because I was at the heart of the preparations for it although I felt more like a victim. The plan was to have an item called, 'Ten little nigger boys' after the style of 'Ten green bottles sat upon a wall.' A wall of desks was constructed, fronted by a stretch of sacking coloured in with chalk to look like brickwork. The mechanics of sitting on, and falling off, this wall were worked out. The next problem was how to blacken our faces. Burnt cork should do the trick, the teacher thought. Let's try it on someone. I was the someone who duly had his face smeared with burnt cork. The process took quite a while because the cork had to be returned to the fire several times before my face was considered black enough. The final result was apparently thought to be highly amusing by those who saw it but I was not one of them and the teacher did not see fit to provide a mirror so that I might share in the amusement. Then came the task of removing my make-up, not an easy one in a school with no washing facilities. After much torturous rubbing and scrubbing in the schoolhouse the teacher considered that my face was sufficiently back to normal for my mother to recognise me and I was sent home. The blacking-up of ten of us must have been too daunting a task for the teacher to face for that was the last we heard of 'Ten little nigger boys.'

I can remember only one occasion when we were taken on an outing from Wasbister School. It was a beautiful summer's day and the teacher decided to take us all on the half-mile walk down to the beach at Saviskaill. Any hopes we may have had of playing in the sand or having a paddle were soon dashed once we arrived there. We were led past the sandy part of the beach and had to scramble over rocks till we came to where many large stones had been washed up on the shore. They were almost spherical and measured about seven or eight inches in diameter. The teacher selected one for each of us and it soon became clear that we were to carry these back to the schoolhouse garden. Whatever those stones weighed when we left the shore must have trebled by the time we had completed the journey and had deposited them along the edge of the teacher's garden path. I wonder if any of them are still there.

I can recall two occasions when my father arranged for me and others in the family to get out of school for the afternoon. We all trooped up to the peat hill away above Langskaill to spread out the peats that had been cut some weeks earlier. By that time some moisture had drained out of the slabs of wet peat which had been stacked on edge at the time of cutting. Our task was to spread them out on the heather to allow further drying out especially on the upper side. At that stage most of the peats were still quite soft, with the consistency of dough, and we could squelch our fingers into them to our hearts' content. At a later date we would return to set them back up on edge in groups of three or four to let the wind blow through them and complete the drying process.

On these occasions we had our tea in the hill from a basket of goodies our father had carried from home. A cloth was spread out on the heather, our cups were filled with milk or with tea and we polished off the contents of the basket. I always thought that tea made in the peat hill with peaty flavoured water tasted even better than the tea at home made with good spring water. After tea another hour's work saw the job finished and we still had enough energy left to run pell mell down the hill through the knee-deep heather on the way home. Such deep, springy and sweet-smelling heather would make a perfect bed if one had to spend a night out-of-doors. I regret never having put it to the test in my younger days.

Every winter the rough roads leading up to the peathill became damaged through water running down them in torrents. Before peats could be carted home the men of the district spent a day or two carrying out repairs to the roads. That was just one of the tasks that had to be done in order to have a stack of peats as winter fuel. Very few Rousay people now consider all the work involved worthwhile and most have switched to other fuels.

Across from the school is the farmhouse of Cogar, occupied, when I was at school, by Robert Inkster and his sister Mary Ann. In those days men did not usually undertake such household tasks as baking if there was a woman in the house but Robert was somewhat different in his ways. One day, as we were leaving school, Mary Ann came out to the front of the house and, much to our amusement, called to her brother who was some distance away.

'Bobby, buddo, come in and bake twa-three scones for tea.'

Some years ago I happened to hear a news item on the radio to the effect that the government was scrapping the requirement for people who brewed ale at home to have a licence to do so. It was stated that in the previous 12 months only 495 licences had been issued in Scotland, 492 of them in Orkney. I do not know whether this surprising statistic indicated that Orcadians had a greater fondness for home brewed ale than people elsewhere, but I do not know a single Rousay person, let alone 492 in Orkney as a whole, who would have let the need for a licence stand between him and the brewing of a kirn of ale.

Quite a lot of brewing went on in Rousay when I was a boy. I once heard a Wester worthy remarking after a drink of ale, 'Man, that stuff's both maet and drink.' My mother brewed once a year, in time for the peat cutting. It must have been very thirsty work for several dozen bottles, carefully packed in a bushel measure, were taken to the hill on peat cutting day. Bobby of Cogar was said to brew a very potent ale. It was claimed to give those who drank it what in modern jargon is called a 'high', but they invariably discovered later that Bobby's brew also produced a 'low' in the form of its highly unpleasant purgative effects.

The Inksters had a brother, John, who was a minister in Toronto, on the shores of Lake Ontario. On a visit home to Rousay, he was invited to conduct a service in the Sourin Kirk. After the singing of the opening psalm the visitor told the shocked congregation that if David had heard his psalms sung like that he would have taken them away from them. It is said that the precentor who had led the singing was much put out by this comment on his performance.

On another occasion John and his Canadian wife were spending a holiday at Cogar. They visited some friends at one of the hillside crofts one day, and as they were leaving to return to Cogar they commented on the beauty of the loch down in the centre of the district with the reddening evening sky reflected in its calm waters. The lady of the house, full of parochial pride, boasted, 'Of course, you won't have such an expanse of water as this where you come from.'

The former Wester school now houses the island's snooker club. There are several other clubs and groups which provide recreation for the present generation of young people. In days gone by, young adults had to find their own amusements which frequently consisted of practical jokes perpetrated on their elders. So it was that a crofter woke up one morning feeling that he had slept long enough. However, it was still dark so he turned over and went back to sleep. During the night he had not heard the visitors who had taken some peats from his stack and had used them to build up the windows of the house, blocking out any light. When he again awoke, daylight had still not appeared. He again tried to get back to sleep but without success and he tossed and turned for what seemed like hours. Eventually he decided he could lie no longer. He rose, pulled on his trousers in the darkness and went to the door. When he looked out he could not believe what he was seeing.

'Maggie, Maggie, come and see this', he called back excitedly to his wife. 'The sun is rising in the west.'

A Wester man, whom we shall call Sandy, was an inveterate practical joker. He spared no one, least of all members of his own family. On one famous occasion he almost came a cropper. He was in Kirkwall for the day and called in at a hall where a one-day sale of household goods was being held. As he entered the crowded room he spotted his mother at the far end busily engaged in examining some of the goods. As she had not seen him he decided to play a little trick on her. He made his way around to near where she was and, when only a yard or two from her, got down on his hands and knees and crawled the rest of the way. When he reached his mother he tickled her on the ankle but she paid no attention. He then tickled her behind the knee. She looked down. It wasn't his mother. Horrified at the mistake he had made in that forest of legs, he crawled away quickly, got to his feet and made his shamefaced escape from the premises as hurriedly as he could.

On another occasion Sandy used his talent for mimicry to have some fun at the expense of his aunt. He phoned her and said, in the local minister's well-known voice, that he would be visiting in the district the following evening and would like to call in at about eight o'clock if that was convenient. He was told that the time would suit very well and that she and her husband would be pleased to see him. Sandy appeared at his aunt's house at half past seven the following evening to find the couple dressed in their Sunday best and the table set with the best china, ready for tea. He pretended not to notice these things as he sat down and started to yarn away as usual. Sandy was in his working clothes which, the couple could not help noticing, gave off the pungent odour of the dung their wearer had been carting out on to the fields that day. His working boots had some suspicious looking splodges adhering to them as well. His aunt was clearly becoming impatient and kept glancing out of the window. Why couldn't he get up and go? Could he not see that they were expecting a visitor? The minister would be there any minute and whatever would he think?

Sandy sat on till after eight watching the couple getting edgier and edgier over his presence but at the same time trying to remain polite to their visitor, unwelcome though he was at that particular time. At last he rose and took his leave, having enjoyed himself immensely.

When he arrived home his wife met him at the door.

'Tak aff thee sharny beuts and that smelly boiler suit afore thoo comes in here. Then go and hiv a bath. And thoo'll need tae hiv anither wan efter thee wark the morn becase the minister his jeust phoned tae say he's coman here on a visit at seven o'clock.'

The road continues past the school, and in front of us is the farm of Innister with its land rising in half a dozen terraces to a ridge 250 feet in height. Beyond the ridge is a large area of rough pasture called the Brings which falls gradually away down to the cliff edge. Innister was my family home and so the Brings formed part of our childhood playground where we could come to no harm provided we stayed away from the cliffs. We were well warned about that danger and, on the whole, were relied upon not to go near them. In time we learned of places along the cliffs where we could descend without much difficulty or danger to favourite fishing spots at Stinkany Geo and Geo Dykesend. The fish we caught were cuithes (young saithe) but sometimes a big ling could be persuaded to take the bait. On a good evening we could catch as many cuithes as we cared to carry home. Those that were not eaten fresh were split and sun dried for later consumption.

Fish formed a large part of our diet at that time. Meat was seldom bought because, coming from Kirkwall, it had lost its freshness by the time it arrived from the van. In any case, much of the meat sent to the islands by the Kirkwall butchers at that time consisted of the poorest cuts that no one in the town would buy. There was fresh pork when a pig was killed each year and the rest of it was salted down

A view of the cliffs at the Brings, looking west from Why Geo. The Lobust, a massive sea stack, can be seen a short distance west of the Quandal Dyke. Behind the Lobust are the cliffs at Hellia Spur. (*Photograph by Willi Murray.*)

for eating later. Not only did we eat fresh and dried cuithes but also salted cod which had been split and sun-dried. They were as hard as boards when bought from the van, and would keep for a long time provided no dampness got to them. When they were being boiled the water had to be changed several times to get rid of the salt. Salted cod, served with potatoes and melted butter, made an excellent meal. Another of my favourites was salted herring. A small barrel of them was bought in the autumn and that provided many a tasty dinner throughout the winter. Every year lots of chickens were hatched on the farm. Most of the cockerels were not wanted but it was very often difficult to identify them until their combs started to grow. By that time they had eaten quite a lot of food so they were kept for a few more weeks to provide some tasty dinners. I quickly tired of chicken day after day but never complained about an unvaried diet of fish.

Every time I hear the song 'All in the April Evening', my mind goes back to an April evening in the Brings when I was about seven years old. It was lambing time and I had gone with my father as he made his evening round of the sheep. The setting sun was reddening the sky

Fishing for cuithes at Stinkany Geo. A simple 'wand', consisting of an eight-to ten-foot long bamboo pole fitted with perhaps four to six hooks, was traditionally used for this type of fishing. (*Photograph by Willi Murray.*)

and for once there was not a breath of wind. The only sounds to be heard were the plaintive bleating of the lambs and the anxious cries of the peewits as we neared their nests. Now, nearly 70 years later, on the rare occasions when we get a very calm, balmy evening like that in the early part of the year, I recall, with a feeling of great yearning, that magical April evening, and I long to be back. In a large family such as ours it was rarely possible for any one child to monopolise a parent's attention for a lengthy period and that evening in the Brings was the only occasion that I can recall having my father all to myself. The beauty of the setting, and the pleasure I felt in his company must have made a strong impression upon my young mind because it has remained with me throughout my life to become one of my fondest memories of childhood. He died a few years later when I was ten years old.

Over 100 years ago an old man in Rousay recorded an account of something that had happened in the Brings when he was young in the early 1800s:

About the commencement of the century, a child by the name of Mowat, about two years old, strayed from the house of Mears in Sourin in a thick mist. His parents sought him for two days in vain. A dog belonging to Furse was missed the same day as the child went away. The dog came home on the third day and got some food. He went away as soon as he had taken it. He was followed by the servant man. The dog ran to a pigsty in the Brings, and when the man went to the sty the dog made for springing at him. He looked in and found the child alive and well. He took the child home and went and told the parents who gladly came for him. He lived in Rousay to an old age. I knew him well. The most remarkable thing about it was that before the dog would venture home for food he had sent all the swine about a mile from the sty in which the child was found.

For most of the year my father's sheep grazed in the Brings but for a period in the winter they were on grass on lower ground. When I was a small boy about five or six years of age my father had a ram that was always described as being uem. 'Uem' is an old Orkney word meaning 'mad', but to us a ram that was uem was one that was likely to charge us if we happened to go anywhere near him. I was crossing a field one day to where my father and another man were laying a drain. The sheep, with the uem ram in their midst, were in that field as well so I was keeping an eye on him in case he started moving in my direction. When he spotted me he started towards me and I began to run. My father, seeing what was happening, ran towards me too but the ram reached me first and butted me hard on the backside sending me flying through the air to land on my face in a welter of tears and high dudgeon. Some time later that ram broke through a boundary fence and got into a fight with a neighbour's ram which died as a result. He then tried to dispose of another neighbour's ram in the same way but this time he got his comeuppance and was himself killed. Served him right, I thought, for what he had done to me.

Grim tales are told of some dark times in Wester's past. Two of them concern shipwrecks. The first story tells of a man from the island of Westray who had taken some cattle to the market in Kirkwall. He was on his way back home feeling well pleased with the prices he had got for his beasts when a storm arose. It is not known whether the boat was lost and he managed to scramble ashore to die shortly afterwards, or whether he was drowned and was later washed ashore on Rousay. Near Grithin, a little rocky bay at the back of Sketquoy, are two stones which are said to mark the head and foot of the Westray man's grave. At a nearby house, also called Grithin, there lived a man Inkster who never had two pennies to rub together. It is said he was never short of money after the unfortunate Westray man came ashore, almost on to his doorstep.

The other shipwreck took place at Saviskaill in 1783. Subsequent happenings on the island must have aroused suspicions in official quarters because a man with seafaring experience was sent from Stromness to Rousay to make enquiries and to report. He found the stranded vessel to be one of 33 tons which had been carrying a cargo of brandy, gin, and tea. All the cargo had been removed from the vessel before his arrival but he saw about 50 casks which were still on the scene. Some were offered to him on sale but he declined to buy. In the house of Alexander Marwick of Saviskaill the investigator saw two books lying on a window ledge. Both books were soaking wet from seawater and he suspected they had come from the stricken ship. Not so, replied Marwick. Both books were his and had got wet when they fell into a tub of water. Marwick did admit having some casks of spirits and the captain's chest in which he had found six ruffled shirts, a half guinea in gold, a pair of silver buckles and a silver watch. Taking possession of these items from the ship must have troubled him less than having the water-soaked books.

About 100 people were busy breaking up the ship. Among them were Alexander Marwick, his son William and his cousin David. The investigator warned them that they would be called to account for their actions but he was told that the wreck was God's send and that coming between them and such divine providence was no business of his. He considered it prudent, 'being a stranger in the place', to say no more. Several people told the investigator that Alexander Marwick was the first to discover the wreck and that one member of the crew, although found floating in the water, had still been breathing. 'For the sake of the wreck', it was alleged Marwick gave the man no assistance and allowed him to die.

Whether by divine action or otherwise, back in the early 1930s, a large quantity of timber came ashore from a ship that had either sunk or had lost its deck cargo. Much of it was washed up below the cliffs along the northwest edge of the Brings making access to it both difficult and dangerous. In one instance, a boy of 14 was lowered to the rocks beneath the cliff on a rope of uncertain quality made up from a ram's tether and some other bits and pieces. He secured a number of battens together and they were hauled to the top. This was repeated several times before he had to be snatched back up to escape the advancing tide.

There were plenty of places around a farm where battens could be conveniently hidden away from the gaze of the Receiver of Wrecks who interested himself in such matters and was wont to demand some payment from those who shared in this bounty of the sea. Stories are told of earlier finds when planks were concealed for a short time under the furrows of a newly ploughed field. Others could lie unseen beneath piles of straw in the inner recesses of the barn until official interest in them had died down. Many a building in Rousay has rafters made from that timber thrown up on the island's shores 60 years ago.

Below Innister the road takes a 90-degree turn and heads uphill towards the southwest. The house of Tou, a short way up the brae, is the home of the island's oldest woman, Annabella Clouston. She is 92 years old and has lived at Tou since her marriage 70 years ago. Despite her age, Annabella is a woman of spirit and greatly enjoyed the thrill of a helicopter flight over Rousay on her 90th birthday. She is a person of gentle manner, quick to praise, eager to understand and slow to condemn, a willing listener and a wise counsellor. One visitor from the south was heard to remark that if he had a granny like that he would 'spoil her rotten'. Like many others, he had come away from Tou treasuring some gem of wisdom as a gift from Annabella.

Beside the road near Tou stand the ruins of an old smiddy which was still in use when I was a boy. The blacksmith was wont to work till late at night and consequently his smiddy was often the meeting place for a few of the neighbouring farmers who gathered of an evening to discuss local affairs and to set the world to rights. At the end of one such evening the first to leave remarked that he would need to be making for home as he had still to wash his face before going to bed. When he added that he had not washed his face for two days it prompted one of the others to exclaim, 'Two days! I haven't washed mine for three weeks, aye, three weeks.'

Up the brae from the smiddy the road levels out as it approaches Wester's boundary with the Westside. The boundary is marked by

Annabella Clouston (front), pictured with members of her family in 1998. Standing (left-to-right): Edna Penny (daughter), Amy Sutherland (great-granddaughter), Ann Sutherland (granddaughter). (*Photograph courtesy Edna Penny.*)

a stone dyke which stretches away into the heather on both sides of the road. There must have been a slap, or a gate, across the road at one time for near this point are the ruins of an old house always referred to as The Slap. The old woman who lived in it 100 years ago was Isabella Craigie, better known as 'Bell o' the Slap'. She was reputed to be well versed in the black arts of witchcraft and those who crossed her were in danger of having a curse called down upon their heads.

The Inkster family who were in Innister at that time, and who were about to flit to Nigley in Evie, had fallen foul of her in some way. On the day of the flitting they were making their way towards Frotoft from where a steamboat was to convey them and their belongings across to Evie. As they approached the Slap they spied old Bell moving about on the road.

'She's crossed the road twice', observed Mrs Inkster to her husband. Being a Caithness woman, she knew about such things.

'That's no a good sign, I can tell thee', she added, shaking her head slowly.

Not a word was exchanged as they drew level with Bell at the side of the road glowering at them from beneath the black shawl pulled low over her eyes.

'That wis no a good sign', repeated Mrs Inkster. 'I dread what this day will bring.'

As the boat took them across the Sound a sudden, violent storm blew up, making it impossible to land on the Evie shore. The storm raged all that day and all that night but shortly after daybreak it eased off and the Inksters, along with their stock and all their belongings were safely landed after a terrifying night at sea fearing for their lives. When they arrived up at Nigley they found that every window in the house had been blown in, such had been the violence of the storm. Later, Bell o' the Slap gloated over what had happened and was heard to claim that if she had crossed the road a third time in the path of the departing Inksters the boat and all aboard would have perished.

'Aye, every wan o' them', she added grimly.

A few hundred yards to the east of the Slap stands the small croft of Deithe, the home of Hugh Craigie. He was a joiner by trade and a highly skilled craftsman by all accounts whose work can still be seen in many houses in the island. Each district could support one or two joiners because their services were needed not only when new buildings were going up but on many other occasions as well. They made farm carts and wheelbarrows, were glaziers and undertakers, and many of them could also turn their hands to making household furniture such as tables, chairs, and cupboards. When a new house was erected the local joiner made all the windows and doors, items which nowadays are often made in a factory and bought in by the builder.

When I was a child most boys wore sturdy leather boots that could stand up to a great deal of rough wear and tear. When mine needed repairs the work was done by my father who must have acquired the skill in his younger days. The island had several cobblers at that time but a generation earlier there had been those who had the skill to make boots and shoes as well as to repair them. Like many rural craftsmen, the shoemakers disappeared from the scene when their services were no longer required as good, factory-made footwear became available at modest prices.

THE WESTSIDE

A mile after leaving Wasbister the road turns southwards around the shoulder of Mansmass Hill. From here there is a splendid view over Quandal and its deserted crofts as well as across Evie Sound to the island of Eynhallow and beyond to Costa Head on the Mainland. It was from this point that the old track that came by Kirkgate in Wasbister and over the hill led in a straight line down the slope to the kirk at Skaill standing on the shore facing Eynhallow.

I was once told a story which is almost beyond belief about an incident that was supposed to have taken place at this point on that old track a long, long time ago, in the days before there was a proper road running round the island. An old woman had died at one of the small crofts on the Wasbister hillside and she was to be buried in the Westside kirkyard beside her late husband. It was a warm summer's day and the men who were carrying the coffin in relays were feeling hot and uncomfortable in their heavy home-spun suits after the long trudge over the rough track. They decided to have a short rest before descending the hill to the kirkyard. The coffin was set down and the men sat down for a breather. They were sitting there talking when they heard a knocking sound coming from the coffin. They looked first at it and then at each other unable to believe what they were hearing. Then the chief mourner, quicker thinking than the others, responded to the ever increasing volume of knocking by taking out his knife and starting to prise up one of the boards that formed the lid of the roughly made coffin. Within a few minutes the whole lid was off and the old woman sat bolt upright and looked about her. When she realised that she was witnessing her own funeral she leapt up, grabbed one of the boards of the lid and started to lay about her like someone demented, shouting, 'Ah'm no deid! Ah'm no deid!' That fact was plain for everyone to see and no one felt inclined to dispute her claim, especially while she wielded the piece of wood. The hapless mourners kept their distance until the poor woman calmed down. After a hurried conversation with the chief mourner she agreed to resume her seat in the coffin. She was conveyed back to her home amid much banter and good cheer.

When the company reached the old woman's cottage the coffin was set down at her door and she was helped to her feet. She turned to the chief mourner and said, 'Next time thoo taks me tae the kirkyard I want thee tae stop at the sam place as thoo did the day. I want thee tae deu that even if hid's poorin wae rain. Juist tae mak sure, thoo kens. Aye, juist tae mak sure.' That instruction was complied with a few years later, I was told, but on that occasion no knocking was heard and the journey continued down to the kirkyard at the shore.

High cliffs face the west along most of the Quandal shoreline. Massive waves roll in after a severe storm at sea to be hurled against these cliffs with a resounding crash that can be heard miles downwind. There is a tidal race, called a 'roost', on each side of Eynhallow, created under certain tide and wind conditions. Angry, white-topped billows appear, a foaming, tempestuous mass of water giving the impression that the sea is boiling. This can be happening while the water round about lies relatively calm and peaceful.

Eynhallow supported a population of 25 until the middle of the nineteenth century when the last of its inhabitants left. They lived on five small holdings which occupied the whole island. It has always been known as a holy island because of a chapel there dating back to Celtic times. It is now a recognised bird sanctuary which is the annual nesting place of a 57-year-old fulmar that is claimed to be the oldest bird in the world. It was thought to be about seven years old when it was first ringed on Eynhallow in 1946.

It is said that the mysterious, vanishing island of Hether Blether lies near Eynhallow. The story goes that long ago a young Rousay woman disappeared and could not be found anywhere despite a long search by her father and brothers. One day, years later, when they were out fishing near Eynhallow a thick mist came down blocking out all the landmarks that normally would show them their way back home. They remained at sea all night and when daybreak came they found that

Eynhallow, from Ward Hill, with Evie and Costa in the background. (*Photograph by Willi Murray.*)

the mist had lifted and that they were near an island that they did not recognise. They went ashore on a beautiful sandy beach where they were met by the long-lost daughter and sister. She told them that she was happily married here on the island of Hether Blether and had three children. She took them to her house and there was great rejoicing. When it came time for the fishermen to leave the father asked his daughter to go with them but she replied that she could not leave her husband and children. However, she gave her father a steel stake and told him that he could return to Hether Blether at any time provided that he was carrying the steel in his hand. Unfortunately, on the way back to Rousay the steel stake was inadvertently lost overboard and was never seen again.

Hether Blether still appears from time to time but not many remain who will claim to have seen it. It has for long been known that if anyone is holding steel in his hand when he first catches sight of the island on one of its rare appearances and succeeds in making his way there and landing on its shore while still clutching the steel, then Hether Blether will vanish no more.

All the land on this side of Rousay belongs to Westness, the island's biggest farm, which extends to over 2,900 acres with about 10 per cent of it being arable land. Forty families that used to live in this district were evicted from their crofts in the middle of the nineteenth century in order to extend this farm to its present size. The best of the land so acquired was squared off and surrounded with stone dykes to provide a few additional fields for Westness. All the rest became rough pasture.

At many points close to the Westside road can be seen remnants of the old hill dykes which separated the common land on the higher ground from the arable land lower down. Most of them follow the contours of the land at a height of 200–250 feet above sea level. In the old days, those who farmed the arable land had grazing rights on the common. These dykes which are much older than most of the stone dykes now seen on the island were built of turf and were commonly referred to as feelie dykes. They were built from material dug from the land near where they stood. To have been effective they must have stood at least four or five feet high and would have required very frequent repairs. Stone, although plentiful enough, provided a dyke that needed little in the way of maintenance but in some instances the stones had to be transported quite a distance to where they were required. This would have been a very difficult task until carts appeared on the island in about 1830, so most of the stone dykes in Rousay are little more than 150 years old. Long stretches of the feelie dykes, now reduced to grassy ridges a foot or two in height, can still be seen snaking across the rough pasture land in many parts of Rousay.

On a grey, sunless day Rousay's stone buildings and dykes can appear rather dull and uninteresting, lacking in colour. However, if they are viewed in bright sunlight they are seen to have a variety of colourings and textures that are not only attractive in themselves but which also blend in naturally with the landscape. The dykes we see here are built without the aid of mortar or any other binding material. The skill of the masons who built them ensured that they would not readily collapse if left undamaged by human hand.

Before cement came on the scene lime was used as a binding agent in housebuilding. Earlier still, clay was commonly used and can be found in many buildings which are still standing. Building with stone is now too expensive for most people and consequently, most new buildings are constructed with pre-cast concrete blocks. Keeping to a vertical or horizontal line must be much easier for present day builders using squared blocks than it was for the stonemasons of bygone days building with irregularly shaped stones. The stonemason also requires much more time for the task than the block builder does. However, it is good to see stone still being used for garden dykes and decorative features in new buildings.

Rousay abounds in prehistoric sites of archaeological interest, with over 100 recorded so far. It is likely that some have been lost to us for ever by farming operations while others lie beneath the soil still hidden from our gaze. Less than a third of those on record have been examined through either complete or partial excavation. The variety of structures found includes brochs, burial cairns, standing stones, Norse burial cists, earth-houses, burnt knowes, and Celtic chapels.

The two best known and most visited of the island's ancient monuments stand within a few yards of each other on the Westside shoreline. They are the Midhowe Broch and the Midhowe Stalled Cairn. The broch, a fortified and protected structure, was built as a place that could be retreated to in times of danger. It dates back about 2,500 years to the time of the Picts. It was excavated in the early 1930s and it was at that time also that the protective seawall was constructed in front of it. This semi-circular seawall is a remarkable structure of five-inch thick slabs of rock set on edge on the rocky foreshore like giant books on a shelf. It slopes inwards for most of its height and outwards for the topmost two feet. Both the broch itself and this seawall rampart, built to protect it from the ferocity of the heavy seas that strike this side of the island, bear witness to the skill and craftsmanship of Orkney stonemasons working on the same site 2,500 years apart.

A stone's throw from the broch is the stalled cairn, a burial place dating back about 5000 years to the time of the Stone Age people. When it was excavated in the early 1930s it was found to be a building over 100 feet long and over 40 feet in width. The walls are a massive 18 feet thick leaving the interior as a long narrow chamber only a little over seven feet wide and varying in height from four to seven feet. Down each side of a narrow central passage the chamber is divided into 12 compartments by flagstones set on edge, giving an appearance very similar to that of a cow byre. It was in these compartments or stalls that the remains of 25 bodies were found, all on one side of the passageway. The bones of some animals and birds were also found. This stalled cairn was considered so important a find that a stone

The Midhowe Broch. The sea wall, which protects the broch at high tide, was built by Stanley Gibson, a local stonemason, assisted by Peemo Smith and Willie Grieve. It is a fine example of the quality of Stanley's workmanship. (*Photograph by Willi Murray.*)

building with overhead lighting and an overhead viewing gangway was erected over it to protect it from further decline.

A short distance along the shore from Midhowe stands the old farmhouse of Brough, the abode of a Craigie family that had considerable standing in the island at one time. The land of this farm was absorbed into the large farm of Westness along with all the other farms in this district in the middle of the nineteenth century. The house has remained empty for the past 100 years and is now roofless but the walls still stand straight and square, a tribute to the craftsmanship of the stonemason who built them.

Nearby, and also on the shoreline, we come upon the old farm buildings of Skaill, a name that points to this having been the residence of an important person in Norse times, someone of power and substance. Such a person of eminence was Sigurd of Westness and it is likely that this was his home.

The most recent excavations in this area were made in 1963. They were sparked off by a farmer coming upon a stone-lined grave whilst digging a hole in which to bury a cow. Experts were called in and the grave was identified as belonging to Norse times. Excavations were carried out on behalf of the National Museums of Scotland and later

Sigrid Kaland, working in the Westness Viking tomb, in 1968. (*Photograph by Bill Murray.*)

by a team from Bergen University. What was revealed was not just one grave but a whole cemetery dating from Pictish times back in the fifth century through to Norse times in the ninth century. The grave accidentally uncovered by the farmer was a Viking one, the burial place of a young woman and a newborn child. In common with many other Viking graves, this one contained a wealth of grave-goods among which was a silvergilt ringed pin with gold filigree and inlaid amber. It is thought to have been made in Scotland in the eighth century, identifying it as a piece of Celtic jewellery which eventually found its way into the grave of a pagan Viking lady. This has come to be known as the Rousay brooch. It is now housed in an Edinburgh museum. Beautiful replicas of it are made and sold by local silversmiths.

Also excavated by the Norwegians at the Westness site were a boat noust and a farmstead both of which date from Norse times.

It is indeed remarkable that on a short half-mile stretch of the Westside shore can be seen evidence of all the different peoples who, through thousands of years past, have gone before us on this island. They stretch back to the Stone Age people who are thought to have been the first inhabitants of Orkney. Many centuries later came the

Picts who built the brochs, to be succeeded about 1200 years ago by the Norsemen about whom most is known by virtue of their being the most recent arrivals. Their influence lives on in our language, in our placenames, in our folklore and customs, and probably in our very natures. Rousay is fortunate in having within this small area such an abundance of archaeological treasures from which to learn about our past. What a pity it is that, until fairly recently, generations of Rousay children were denied the opportunity of having their minds stimulated by learning at school of the richness of their heritage represented by the island's ancient monuments. It is good that the subject is not being neglected by today's teachers.

Some much needed signposting of these historic sites along the Westness shore has been put in place in recent years. Welcome though this is, it is not sufficient merely to identify the sites. I think that most visitors would wish to be able to learn something about the site to which the signpost has drawn their attention. What is needed is a weatherproof information board at each site. Leaflets and booklets giving the desired information are available at tourist offices and elsewhere but not everyone has the foresight to obtain them prior to setting out, and it would greatly add to the enjoyment of the visit if the information were available on-site.

When excavation took place of archaeological sites in Rousay and many other places in Orkney all the important artefacts found were removed to museums in the south, many of them to the Museum of Antiquities in Edinburgh. At none of the Rousay sites are any of the items unearthed there on exhibit. All have been taken elsewhere, away from the island where they were found to a central museum hundreds of miles away. Would it not be of great interest to visitors to these sites if the artefacts found there were on show nearby, within the county, if not within the island. Tankerness House Museum in Kirkwall has a great many important finds from excavations carried out since it opened but comparatively few from earlier digs such as those on Rousay.

There are strong arguments in support of a national museum having most of the important finds where they can be placed and studied in the context of a collection made up of elements gathered from a much wider area. More people are likely to visit central collections than local ones. There is also the problem of providing in smaller communities adequate housing which would be not only secure but which could also provide for the environmental controls of temperature, humidity and light that are necessary for the preservation of some ancient objects. Moreover, the cost of housing and displaying these treasures in the localities where they were found has to come from local resources whereas the costs of our national museums are paid for by all taxpayers.

It tends to be in the nature of the keepers of our national treasures to want to retain them in central museums and to dismiss high-handedly any suggestion that any of them should be returned, even on a temporary or seasonal basis, to the part of the country where they were found. Most of the artefacts found in the Rousay sites were sent to Edinburgh at the time of discovery because there was no place in Orkney at that time in which to house them properly. I suggest that the time has come when they should be seen more often in Orkney where they would greatly add to the interest of those who come here to visit our ancient monuments.

Down by the shore, in the midst of these prehistoric treasures, stand the ruins of St Mary's Church, the island's first parish kirk. Surrounding it is a small graveyard, one of five in Rousay, two of which are still in use. For anyone researching a family tree, gravestone inscriptions are valuable sources of information as I discovered some years ago when I was piecing together the histories of most of the old Rousay families.° Almost all my traceable ancestors, in one case going back as far as eight generations, lived out their lives in Rousay and lie buried in Rousay soil. My family tree is well and truly rooted in this island.

When I visited this kirkyard recently I noticed the sole of an old boot lying on one of the window sills of the ruined kirk. This brought to mind a story of something that had happened more than 100 years ago. In 1893 the Rousay postboat was lost at sea on its way across from Evie on the Mainland. Its two crewmen, along with the passengers, a mother and three children, were all drowned. The boatmen were buried in the Westside kirkyard. Some weeks after the tragedy the boots of one of them came ashore and were placed on his grave where they remained for a great many years, gradually mouldering away. It is likely that the tackety sole I saw is all that now remains of that boatman's boots.

°*Rousay Roots*, Third Edition, 1999. Robert C. Marwick.

Down through the years, Rousay people, like other islanders have had to endure loss of lives resulting from boating accidents. These occurred although most islesmen were skilled in boatmanship. Nowadays, such accidents may be less frequent because boats are bigger with powerful engines, and are equipped with more safety equipment.

One of the worst such disasters around Rousay occurred in 1861 when four young men in a sailing boat were returning to Wyre after taking some grain across to the meal-mill at Hullion.It was a beautiful day and the sea was at peace. Near the Wyre shore a man climbed the mast to clear a blocked pulley. It is not known if his weight at that height capsized the boat or if he fell into the water and the others made vain attempts to rescue him. Their shouts were heard from shore and a boat put off to the rescue but all four men were lost.

Westness is a large farm, and in addition to other stock, carries a flock of about 1,200 sheep. Sixty years ago the farmer there paid £40 for a sheepdog of good breeding. This was at a time when a farm worker earned £10 for a half-year's work. His neighbours thought he had gone crazy paying so much for a mere dog. The farmer's reply was to ask where he could have found a man to do all that running for a one-off payment of £40 and one meal a day.

The first dog I remember at home was a collie named Tweed. He had the colouring of a Shetland collie of today but was a much bigger dog than most of that breed. He had grown old by the time when I first remember him and was no longer being called upon to do much work around the farm. Eventually he had to go but my father could not bring himself to shoot him and called in a neighbour to do it. The next dog to appear on the scene was Peter, another big collie who seemed to be there through most of my childhood days. What a great dog he was. Unlike many of his breed, he would work for anyone, even us children. We had only to yell, 'Peter', and he would come running, eager for any task we had for him. I am glad I was away from home by the time his working days came to an end and he had to go the way of Tweed

Just a stone's throw from the buildings at Westness Farm stands Westness House which used to be the residence of the island's main

landowner. It did not match the pretensions of General Burroughs who came to live there in 1863 and after ten years he moved to a baronial mansion he had had built at Trumland, a few miles away. An extensive refurbishment of Westness House has been carried out by new owners in recent years. This has been done in a way that emphasises the unpretentious elegance of the house. The wooded gardens in which the house is set lie on a south-facing slope and reach down to the beach. Near the west wall of the garden stands a small chapel dating from the 1920s when it was created from the boiler house that served the greenhouses in earlier times. A nineteenth-century visitor to Westness was greatly impressed by the display he found in these greenhouses. In his *Summers and Winters in the Orkneys*, David Gorrie wrote in 1869:

> It excites surprise that the remote and hilly regions of Rousay can produce grapes, and the wealth of flowers in the hothouses might startle strangers.

Jeemie Low was a gardener there for many years. He was a very pious man and conducted Sunday schools in Frotoft and Wasbister on alternate Sundays. I was one of his pupils when I was a small boy. Reputedly, Jeemie could not sing so he had an assistant in the person of old Robbie Sinclair of Sketquoy who had a good voice for leading the singing. Robbie's Sunday suit was made of a thick tweed with a herring bone pattern. That weight of cloth is seen nowadays only in a very heavy winter overcoat.

Robbie had another duty in addition to leading the singing. Each of us had a small blue-covered book showing a biblical text and a lesson for each Sunday. The inside back cover was marked off in boxes for recording our attendances. It was Robbie's duty to carry out this task. Everything about Robbie was big, it seemed to me. He was a big man with a big, deep, sonorous voice but most noticeable were his hands. To me they looked like the hands of a giant. He would lay my tiny book open on his huge palm, reach into his waistcoat pocket and bring out between finger and thumb a one-inch stub of indelible pencil. He would then wet the point on his tongue and solemnly place a X in the appropriate box. Then with equal solemnity the book would be handed back to me. It always amazed me that such huge hands could perform such a finicky task.

In the summer Jeemie held a Sunday School picnic for his pupils from both districts. We were transported over to Westness in carts, the longest 'hurl' most of us had during the year. We particularly liked the races Jeemie and his helpers had arranged for us because the money prizes were always greater than those handed out at the day-school picnic. After the sports programme had been completed we had a picnic tea before being taken on a tour of the garden at Westness House. To us that garden was a place of delight. It had trees, real trees. We stood and gazed in wonder. We had never before seen trees except in pictures. And there was a strange bird called a peacock which fanned its tail to its full glory just for our benefit. I remember a wooden summer-house that revolved on its base so that it could always face the sun. Jeemie Low shepherded us through these delights, all the time smiling benignly upon us. He was a kind and gentle man who sought no reward for his good works.

FROTOFT

As we leave Westness the road changes direction slightly to make its way through Frotoft and along the south side of the island. This is the part of Rousay that I know least well because I have never lived in it and for many years most of my visits there were of a fleeting nature based mainly on the comings and goings of Tom Sinclair's postboat. Tom, like his father before him, ran the postboat and passenger service across to Evie on the Mainland for many years. The weather had to be very rough to stop Tom crossing. If he donned his heavy yellow oilskins before setting out, the passengers knew it would be prudent to remain under the decked-in section of the boat. Tom would stand in the open stern beside the tiller seemingly unmindful of the conditions as the wind lashed spray across his rough-hewn features.

In addition to his regular runs, Tom was also available for hires, some of which were requested at inconvenient, and even unreasonable, times. A hire that I once requested fell into the latter category. It was shortly after the war ended and I was on my way home after three years in the Far East. I had reached Orkney on a Saturday afternoon in May but I tarried too long on the Mainland and thoughtlessly did not phone Tom till eight o'clock in the evening. He told me he had just arrived home after a long day boating sheep to Eynhallow. While he did not actually refuse to cross it was clear that he thought that I was asking too much in expecting him to make another crossing at that late hour. I have to admit that I then took advantage of Tom's good nature by complaining that it was hard lines to have come half way round the world to find myself stuck on the last mile. That did it. He agreed to cross for me, and it is to his credit that he could not have been more pleasant when he greeted me on the Evie shore.

Tom Sinclair (senior) *c.* 1930. (*Photograph courtesy Muriel Johnston.*)

Tom Sinclair (junior) *c.* 1940. (*Photograph courtesy Muriel Johnston.*)

Tom Sinclair, and his boat, pictured at the Yorville pier in 1961.

Billo and Clara Grieve, from Furse, are helping Mrs Dalling, a visitor to the island, onto the boat. Mr and Mrs Dalling's visit was a particularly sad one. Their son, Bill, a keen birdwatcher, fell to his death from the cliffs near the Lobust. They came to the island to visit the spot where the accident happened. (*Photograph courtesy Bill and Freda Murray.*)

Tom had inherited the ferryman's job from his father, also called Tom. In his later years Tom senior bought a car and learned to drive. There was a steep banking from the front of his house down to the main road. One day when he had his small grandson as a passenger old Tom misjudged things and the car went over the edge and rolled over several times before coming to rest the right way up on the road below. The wee lad looked at his grandfather admiringly and said, 'Do that again, Grandad.'

A Frotoft man whom I first met when I was a boy was George Reid of Tratland whose father had been one of the postboat crew who lost their lives in the 1893 tragedy. George and Tom Sinclair senior ran the postboat for many years and George still had a motor boat when I first knew him. He had a wonderful sense of humour and always seemed to have a twinkle in his eye It amused me as a child that he always wore his cap so far forward on his head that it left a half moon of baldness exposed at the back.

George Reid. (*Photograph courtesy Olive Kemp.*)

To mark the coronation in 1937, we had been given a few days off school but I had no way of getting home to Rousay from Kirkwall. I was lucky enough to meet George who happened to be in from Rousay on his boat. He readily agreed to my request for a passage home and instructed me to be at a certain point on the pier at 10 o'clock that night. I was old enough to know that the time I had been given coincided with the closing of the pubs. However, it was almost mid-summer and the light was still good at that time of night. I made sure I was at the pier in good time. George and two companions duly appeared and we set off. The three men sat at the stern keeping themselves warm with frequent swigs from a bottle of whisky but I sheltered from the chill of the sea breeze under the small foredeck. As we neared Rousay George came forward to where I was sitting and began searching for something among the parcels he had placed there. At last he found what he was looking for and handed me a pear, with the injunction that I was not to tell anyone he and his companions had been drinking in the boat. I would learn later that, boat or no boat, George liked his dram, and everyone knew it. But I liked George, and

The shop at Hullion *c.* 1975. The proprietor, Dave Gibson, (standing behind the counter) is seen with his daughter, Julia Peace, and her baby, David Peace. The customers are Norman and Hilda Reid. (*Photograph courtesy Edith Gibson.*)

his secret was safe with me. Besides, had he not given me a passage home, and a pear into the bargain?

The last time I saw George was ten years later at a ploughing match in Wester. As a member of the Royal Highland Agricultural Society he had a duty to visit the field to see that the contest was being conducted according to the Society's rules. He arrived on the field in high spirits after enjoying a lunch which obviously had had a high liquid content. Spotting an old friend, George cheerfully announced his presence with, 'Beuy, Jock, I'm jeust as happy as a pig in sh—.' George was a delightful man to know. What a pity it is that there are not more of his kind around today.

A shop at Hullion, in the middle of the district, served the people of Frotoft and other parts of Rousay for many years. It closed down recently after having been in operation on that site from at least as far back as the early 1800s. The island's main Post Office was also at Hullion for many years, with smaller ones at Sourin and Wasbister. Each district had its own postman until the mid-1930s when a mail

A young Dave Gibson, and his older brother, Bill, with Hullion's horse-drawn shop and delivery van *c.* 1935. This was one of three horse-drawn vans operating in Rousay in the 1930s. The other two belonged to the Co-op in Sourin, and to Willie Marwick at the pier. (*Photograph courtesy Tommy Gibson.*)

van came to the island and one postman could cope with all the deliveries except those in Sourin which were covered on foot by Charlie Flett, a local worthy. One day Charlie was on his rounds when he was met on the road by someone driving three or four cattle which had strayed. He asked Charlie if the animals were his. Charlie put his arms around the neck of one cow and said, 'Bogle noo, bonie ting.' The cow bellowed and Charlie nodded. 'Yes, they're mine', he replied, and continued on his way.

Many years earlier, James Clouston had been the postman in Wester and when he retired a public collection was taken up to buy him a present. This happened just about the time that I had to go into hospital to have my tonsils removed. My mother took me into Kirkwall on the steamer on Monday morning and straight up to the hospital. There she was told that the operation could not be performed that day as I had eaten too much for breakfast. No more than a thin half-slice of toast was all I was to have in the morning. Next morning, after that meagre breakfast, I was admitted and put to bed. Eventually a big nurse appeared and put a nightgown on me. She then added insult to injury by picking me up and carrying me through to the

Hullion's Austin van, which served as a mobile shop from the early 1960s to the mid 1970s. Latterly, Dave Gibson used an estate car to make deliveries (*Photograph courtesy Tommy Gibson.*)

operating theatre. How undignified! I was a big boy of seven and there I was being carried along like a baby, and in a goonie too. I was black affronted! However, I had no time to brood over the affront as the chloroform mask was put on my face and I was told to breathe deeply. I was aware of nothing more until I woke up on a blood-soaked pillow to be told that my mother was there to take me out. I had been in hospital for six hours. A car took us to a friend's house and I was put to bed.

Next morning we went back home to Rousay on the steamer and I was kept in bed for the rest of that day. I lived on saps – bread broken into small pieces in very sweet tea – for several days. That was a favourite of mine which I sometimes made for myself at teatime if my mother was not watching how much sugar I was spooning in. I suppose I was given other soft foods as well such as porridge and milk puddings but saps is the one I remember. I came home from hospital on a Wednesday and on the Friday evening, with others in the family, I was at the school to see James Clouston being presented with a clock. I cannot remember if I got away with being allowed to stay on for the dance that would have followed.

Frotoft's postman for many years was Danny Mackay. He was one of a group of men who had gathered at the Hullion shop one evening. There had been heavy rain and the nearby burn was in full spate. One of the group challenged Danny to leap the burn. Danny considered the matter for a minute and replied that he would be able to do it if he had a glass of whisky inside him. The drink was provided and Danny got ready for the dare. He took a good run at the burn but pulled up at the bank saying he was sure he could do it if he got another whisky. A second glass was produced and downed and Danny got set once more. This time he took a longer run, increased his speed until it looked as if he had enough momentum to take him across but again he pulled up at the edge. He assured his companions that just one more glass would do the trick. They debated the matter for a few minutes before consenting. After downing his third glass Danny removed his jacket, rolled up his shirt sleeves, tucked his trouser legs into his socks and took a very determined run at the burn. It looked as though nothing could stop him this time but he suddenly pulled up at the edge again.

'What's wrong this time?' demanded his friends.

'Boys', replied Danny, 'I doot I've had too much tae drink tae jump the burn the night.'

I wonder if the Post Office still operates a COD (Cash on Delivery) service. It was a system widely used in the 1930s whereby goods bought by mail order could be paid for on delivery by the postman. Firms such as J.D. Williams and Oxendales both of Manchester provided a mail order service, mainly in clothing and footwear, to countless households throughout the Scottish Highlands and Islands. The arrival of these parcels created great excitement among us children on the occasions when we knew they contained something new for us.

Some of Rousay's shopping was done from nearer home. Orkney firms such as P.L. Johnston of Stromness and D.H. Gorn and James Croy of Kirkwall used to send their salesmen on periodic rounds of the islands. With a large suitcase, or perhaps two, strapped to his bike the salesman would make his way from house to house hoping that all the effort would produce a sizeable order. To us country children, who hardly saw a town shop from one year's end to the next, this was a normal way of shopping and we would all gather round as the suitcase was slowly unpacked. Out came pullovers and pillow slips, socks and shirts, blouses and bloomers, towels and ties, frocks and flimsy whatsits, to form an ever increasing pile on the open lid of the case. Swatches of cloth samples were always carried for the benefit of customers who might wish to order a new suit or jacket. I remember one occasion when I was being measured for a suit. I was about 14 at the time and the salesman remarked that in terms of suit size I was neither a boy nor a man. 'He must be a lass', quipped an older brother, much to my angry embarrassment.

Another group of vendors who came around from time to time were the tinkers. Their goods were carried in a pack slung over the shoulder. We considered their sales talk more pungent and amusing than that of the polite, well-spoken salesmen from the town shops, and wondered why they always bestowed on the money a token spit before pocketing it.

The old Frotoft school was the smallest of the three district schools. It was built to replace the original Parish School in the Westside after most of the families had been evicted from their crofts in that part of the island. In each district the school was the focal point for many community activities. It was the venue for meetings, dances, concerts and parties. At least two dances in each district each year were promoted by the school to follow the picnic and sports in summer and the concert and party at Christmas but other dances took place as well at various times. Fifty years ago I used to attend two or three dances every summer when I was home on holiday. I recall how pleasant it was to make my way home from a dance, sometimes by a circuitous route, at two or three o'clock in the morning in good daylight. Nowadays when it is easier to travel further to take part in such community activities there are fewer of them and complaints are heard in the island that it is becoming ever more difficult to persuade young people to take part in them. It is to be hoped that this is due more to the widespread availability of various forms of home entertainment than it is to a weakening of the community bonds that are formed whenever people gather together for a common purpose.

In days gone by, when there were more working farms on the island than there are now, competitions of various kinds were held in which farmers could pit their skills against those of their neighbours. The most important of these was the agricultural show at which farmers had the opportunity of having their animals and stockmanship judged against those of others. Not every farmer took part but among those who did the competition was keen. Cattle formed the largest category in the show but horses and sheep were also well represented, with poultry making an occasional appearance. The first show was held in 1874 and it remained an important annual event in the Rousay calendar until the early 1960s.

A horticultural and crafts show was always held on the same day as the cattle show. The island's gardeners and housewives put on impressive displays of flowers and vegetables, baking of all kinds and home-made jams, sewing and knitting and other handcrafts, as well as butter, cheese and eggs.

The first ploughing match in the island also took place in 1874 and it too became an annual event. This was a competition which farmers' sons and other young ploughmen entered with great enthusiasm. Occasionally a boy as young as 14 years competed and was allowed a day off school to do so. One lad who had competed at that age told me recently that his father had not been keen on his taking part and had been reluctant to set out on a wet and cold winter morning to take the horses and the plough, carried in a cart, around to the field of competition on the other side of the island seven miles away. He did not get a prize for his ploughing that day but he got one for being the youngest ploughman. He related that he returned home full of manly pride at being called a ploughman. To be so called was honour enough for him. Ploughing was a task in which many young men were keen to demonstrate their skills and to be declared the winner at the end of the day was an honour highly thought of and eagerly sought after. Consequently, much earnest practice was put in by young ploughmen in the weeks prior to the contest. The advice of older, more experienced men was sought and given. Frequent visits to the blacksmith might be made if it was considered that last minute adjustments to the plough were necessary.

A turn-out of up to 20 pairs of Clydesdales pulling single-furrow ploughs all working in the same field made an impressive sight. As prizes were also awarded for grooming and harness as well as for ploughing, most entrants took the trouble to add some decoration to their horses by weaving coloured ribbons or raffia into manes and tails, and to polish up their harness leather and metalwork. One or two farmers invested in special show harness which was never used at any other time. They inevitably always won the prizes for the best harness but most could not afford to go to such lengths. One ploughman, who was a regular competitor, was notoriously slower than the others and was always the last to finish. Consequently, he was always awarded the prize set aside for this – a packet of Epsom salts. Eventually tractors became common and replaced teams of horses at ploughing matches but they lacked the appeal of horses and the competition did not survive for much longer.

Another annual competition was the hoeing match. The turnip sowing machines in use when every farm grew turnips sowed a continuous line of seed resulting in the need for the plants to be thinned out when they were a few inches high. Long handled hoes were used and the aim was to leave about six inches between plants and not a weed in sight. Every available person on the farm turned out to help with this task. If the seed had been sown too thickly or if germination had been better than expected the result was too many spindly plants growing together and difficult to separate with a hoe. Another difficulty arose if the hoers could not keep pace with the growth of the crop because the larger the plants the harder it was to push out the unwanted ones. Little wonder that in some farming areas hoes were discarded and the thinning done by hand. Many days were spent on this monotonous task every summer. The hoeing match was always held in the evening after the normal day's work was done. Men, women and children joined in to single a drill or two each but only those who wished to do so entered the competitive section of the field. When the competitors had finished their set tasks they moved to work on another part of the field while the judges got down to the job of drawing up an order of merit. When the evening's work was done everyone moved to the school where supper was served before the prize list was announced. Invariably, the evening ended with a dance.

At that time about 40 per cent of the arable land was given over to growing oats and bere, 20 per cent to turnips and potatoes, and 40 per cent to grass, with hay being taken from half of that. This meant that more than half the arable land had to be ploughed each year. Ploughing used to occupy many weeks every winter and Spring when it all had to be done with horse-drawn single-furrow ploughs. It was begun shortly after harvest. The grass fields in which oats were to be sown were always the first to be ploughed to give time for the turf to be broken down and the weeds to be killed off by the frost before sowing time in the Spring. The fields that had grown oats the previous year were the next to be ploughed. These fields were due to be planted with potatoes and turnips requiring heavy fertilising, so prior to being ploughed large quantities of dung accumulated from the byres during the winter had to be carted out and spread over the stubble. Seaweed, always referred to as ware, was frequently spread on the land as a fertiliser. Some chemical fertilisers were also in use at that time. The turnip and potato fields from the previous year were the last to be ploughed and later they were sown with oats or bere along with grass seed.

More time and effort were put into growing and using turnips than was the case with any other crop. The field in which they were to be grown had to be gone over many times with various implements to break the soil down to a fine enough tilth to receive the seed. Later came the thinning and hoeing, followed a few weeks later by running a horse-drawn implement called a scuffler between the drills to keep down the weeds. All winter, turnips had to be cut from the ground, often when it was frozen, before being loaded on to a cart and conveyed to a shed near the byre where they were carried in basketfuls to the cattle. By the time the winter work with turnips was nearly over the fields for the new crop were already being prepared. It is little wonder that few farmers seem to bother with them nowadays.

Harvesting began with the winning of the hay crop in mid-summer. It was cut with a two-horse reaper, and when dry enough the swathes were gathered together using a horse-drawn rake before being piled into small ricks called coles. At a later stage these were carted into the stackyard to be built into one large stack which was drawn on, as needed, to feed the horses during the winter. Nowadays hay is dealt with in a very different, and less labour intensive, way, being packed into large bales which are then polythene wrapped for storage out-of-doors.

The grain harvest started in September and could last for many weeks depending on the weather. It too was cut by reaper and it required everyone to lend a hand in lifting and binding the sheaves and standing them in stooks to dry. Children helped by making the bands for the sheaves and later graduated to lifting them on to the band ready for binding by a grown-up. The end of crop cutting was referred as 'shearing off' and on many farms was marked by having a plum-duff for tea that day. When the sheaves were dry enough they were carted to the stackyard near the barn where they were built into stacks and secured against winter storms. Sometimes, either because the stackyard was full or simply to save time, some stacks were built in a corner of the field in which the crop had grown. These stacks made ideal homes for rats and mice, giving them warm, snug shelter and a plentiful supply of food to see them through the long winter months. The farm dogs had a field day whenever a stack had to be taken into the barn for threshing and the rodents had to run the gauntlet of their enemies sitting ready to pounce on them as the last of the sheaves uncovered their winter home.

Every farm had a threshing mill of some kind. On a small croft the crop would be threshed on a back-breaking handmill but larger holdings had mills driven by a waterwheel or an engine. I recently heard a 90-year-old retired farmer from Rousay say in a radio discussion that in his lifetime he had seen threshing methods move all the way from the flail, reaching back to biblical times, to the combine harvester of the present day. Some of the grain was sent to the mealmill, some used for stock or poultry feed and a quantity had to be saved for the following year's seed. Cattle ate most of the straw and the oat chaff was used for animal bedding. Another use made of chaff was as a filling for bedsacks made of a closely woven material called ticking, the predecessor of the modern mattress. Anyone who has not slept on a chaff-filled bedsack cannot imagine how comfortable it was when it had been newly filled.

For a long time the eggs from the poultry kept by the farmer's wife helped to pay for the groceries obtained from the island shops and their travelling vans. After the Second World War, egg production expanded rapidly throughout Orkney and most big producers shipped their eggs directly to a grading station which marketed them. At that time eggs accounted for a large part of the income of many farms. The egg boom lasted for about six years. Prices began to fall and Orkney farmers could not compete with the very large producers in the south whose relative costs were much lower. Now, very few poultry are to be seen in the island.

Cattle were taken indoors towards the end of October when the grass had stopped growing and were not put out again until April. All milking was done by hand. Some milk was put through the separator each day and the cream kept for butter-making. When I was a boy every farm produced butter and cheese. Often, when milk was plentiful in the summer months, some of that produce would be sold. Butter-making invariably took place on Saturday afternoon at home and I was sometimes roped in to stand turning the churn for what seemed like hours when I would rather have been doing something of my own choosing. I would stop every few minutes to take yet another look at the small glass circle set into the lid. If it was white the churn still held cream but if the glass had become clear it was an indication that the cream had changed to butter and that I was released to follow my own pursuits.

Other tasks that were carried out on Saturday were the blackleading of the kitchen stove and the washing of the stone floor in the kitchen. At that time every farm kitchen had a square stove about 2 feet high that stood on four short legs. It had a front step under which was the ashpan and the front of the firebox was a set of vertical iron ribs. Behind the firebox was a commodious oven reached by a door at each side, The top had four round lift-off covers to allow for refuelling. Any of these covers could be removed to allow the heat to reach directly on to a pot or kettle. Every farm kitchen had a flagstone floor which was difficult to keep clean. Eventually most of them were removed and replaced with concrete.

At home we always ate far more fish than meat because fresh meat was difficult to get on a small island. A pig was reared every year and fattened up for killing. It was then we had enough fresh pork to weary us and what we did not manage to consume fresh was salted down for future use. I was a long time into adult life before I became reconciled to eating pork again and actually enjoying it.

Our pig was usually killed on a Saturday. This was a peculiar choice of day because, although we children were kept well out of sight of the grisly scene, we could still hear the squeals of the animal as it met its fate. I suppose my father could have carried out the deed if he had had to but I do not recall that he ever did so and a neighbour was called in to do the job. I also remember other neighbours being called in whenever other animals had to be put down by shooting.

During my lifetime and particularly during the past 30 years, vast changes have taken place in farming methods in Rousay. Gone are the horses and the threshing mills. Stables and barns have been converted to byres to accommodate the greater number of cattle being kept. Gone are the pigs and the hens. Gone is much of the hard manual labour now happily passed on to machines. Grass is now the main crop with hay and silage being taken from some of the acres devoted to it. The only grain that is grown is some barley for winter feed. A few farms grow some turnips but most of the labour expended on them in former times is now undertaken mechanically. All these changes have resulted in a great decrease in the number of people needed to work the land. Gone too are the days when a farm of less than 100 acres could support a family without some member of it bringing in additional income. In the island as a whole, only about a dozen farmers are now operating on a significant scale. In addition, there are two or three hobby farmers. Most of the big farmers have bought or rent considerable acreages over and above their original holdings, with the two largest farms,Westness and Trumland, being the main exceptions. All the land in Wester, except for a few derelict crofts, is farmed by only three farmers. When I was a child, about 20 farms and crofts in the district were being worked as separate units. Almost the whole of Frotoft is now farmed by one farmer. However, in that district most of the crofthouses in the lower parts of the district and the houses on the small farms are still occupied.

From the low lying part of Frotoft the road climbs past Cotafea before levelling out for the next mile or so along to Trumland and back down to the pier. Among the cluster of buildings that has sprung up near the pier in recent times are those housing the fish processing plant. This was set up in 1971 to help the local fishing industry and to provide employment in an attempt to halt the depopulation of the island. Mrs Helen Firth, who was at that time the island's representative on Orkney Islands Council, was the moving force in getting this co-operative venture under way. The project, operating under the name Rousay Processors was widely supported by the islanders most of whom bought shares in it. Assistance with funding came from the Highlands and Islands Development Board and later from Orkney Islands Council. It also had the support of the Rousay fishermen, as well as many from other islands, who sold their catches to it. This new venture prospered in its early years and gave employment, some of it seasonal and part-time, to as many as 30 people. It was seen by many as the best thing that had happened to Rousay in a long time.

A management committee elected from the shareholders had overall control of the project but the day-to-day running of the plant was the responsibility of the manager appointed by the committee.

There was a high turnover of managers during the 24 years of the project's life. Many of those appointed lacked the managerial experience that the post called for but the committee could not afford to bring in a manager with the greater expertise required to carry the project forward. Initially, marketing of the plant's produce was done by the Orkney Fishermen's Society but latterly the project took on this task itself. Few of the managers appointed possessed marketing skills. This sometimes resulted in good marketing opportunities being missed by a manager who lacked the experience and vision to respond to changing market requirements. In some cases the marketing practices adopted were inept. Much earnest effort was put in by the committee but it was handicapped by its lack of expertise in that line of business and did not always feel confident enough to exercise the powers of overall control vested in it. The result was that for the most part the manager was given a free hand to run the project as best he could without much guidance or control from above. Although most of the workers were part-timers there were also long term staff who gave very loyal service to the project over many years.

While crab and lobster fetched good prices the project prospered and was able to pay dividends to the shareholders. However the plant was operating only on a part-time basis and was closed during some winters because of the seasonal nature of crab fishing. Having taken on its own marketing, it found itself operating on too small a scale to obtain the best prices in an increasingly competitive market. Consequently it lost much of the support of the fishermen who were able to obtain better prices elsewhere. This coincided with falling prices for crabmeat due to the recession and a general decline in the fishing industry. The resulting decline in the fortunes of Rousay Processors gathered speed and was never halted.

For the project, it has to be said that it provided much needed employment in the island during the 24 years of its life. It had to finish trading in 1995 when, already in debt, it was unable to raise the funds required to upgrade the plant to meet new hygiene regulations required by the EEC.

At a fork in the road just above the pier stands the memorial to the men from the parish who lost their lives in the two world wars. I sometimes stop and look at the list of names and ages. With one or two exceptions, all were young men, some not even out of their teenage years. All but two of them died in the First World War so very few remain alive who knew them, but their names are recorded here to remind us of the dreadful sacrifice they were called upon to make. I think of the quiet, peaceful community from which they came and of the sheer hell they had to endure as they went to their deaths in the carnage and the gore and the mud and chaos of a faraway battlefield. Lions led by donkeys, someone said. I think of the three who all left Rousay on the same day in 1917, all three not long out of their boyhood. They lived within a very short distance of one another and had gone to school together. On the morning of their departure they bade tearful farewells to their families and friends and off they went to fight a war in a distant land. Twelve short weeks later all three were dead. What a waste.

New Orcadians

One hundred and fifty years ago, Pat, shortly before your forebears left the island, Rousay had almost 1000 inhabitants. Now it has only a quarter of that number. By the turn of the twentieth century the population had fallen by over a third to 627 but in the next 50 years that figure almost halved to 342 in 1951. Then the rate of decline speeded up taking half that number away by 1971 when the island's population reached its lowest level at 181.

The first houses to be vacated were some of the small crofts on the hill ground around the fringes of each district. Young people left them to seek a better living elsewhere and when their elders died off the houses were left empty while the land, in many cases, was taken over by neighbouring farms as additional grazing. The rapid mechanisation that took place on farms after the Second World War, and the absence of other forms of employment resulted, during the 1950s and 1960s, in the most rapid decline in population that the island has ever experienced. Lack of work was not the only reason for the exodus. Many farmers moved to larger farms on the Mainland of Orkney or to the rich farmlands of the north-east of Scotland, and it became common for people reaching retiral age to move to the Mainland, mainly into Kirkwall. A poor steamer service, high freight charges, and the lack of mains electricity and other services were all contributory factors.

For many generations it had been the case that very few of the pupils who went on to higher education returned to live in Rousay because there were no job opportunities for them in the island. This problem worsened when all Rousay children had to go to Kirkwall for their secondary education. This tended to give some of them a taste for town life which they were unwilling to give up when their schooldays came to an end.

The population tide turned in the early 1970s when families from the south, mainly from England, began settling in the island. Many came seeking peace and quiet away from the hustle and bustle of city life. Life in the countryside held the promise of contentment, less pressure, greater relaxation, and the satisfaction that comes from owning land. Some saw a move to the country as offering more opportunities for becoming part of the community in a more involved way, while others regarded it as an escape to a quiet and unhurried way of life in which they would find fulfilment. For many, who saw themselves as refugees from the rat race of urban life, an island offered additional attractions such as space and solitude, and freedom to get away from the stresses of overcrowded cities. An added attraction for many of these migrants to Orkney were the low property prices, and Rousay, in particular, offered plenty of properties to choose from in the 1970s and 1980s.

There has been a high rate of turnover among the incomers. People from an urban background who fantasise about the joys and beauties of rural life frequently find that the reality falls far short of their dreams, and ruefully return whence they came. One Orkney winter has been enough for some while others have discovered in a much shorter time that Rousay was not for them and quickly moved on. The turnover among incomers continues. Among those who come are some undesirables who see an island as a bolthole in which to hide from the consequences of their misdeeds elsewhere. When the law eventually catches up with them and their crimes come to light, these people are invariably described in the media as being Orcadians. This practice naturally infuriates native Orcadians who resent the damage it does to Orkney's good name.

It is estimated that almost 300 have come to Rousay in the past 25 years of whom about a half have remained, to form about two-thirds of the island's present population. Among those who appear most settled are those who have invested in farms or other business ventures. Perhaps they have found in Rousay and its way of life what they were seeking when they moved here. It is clear that some of them have come to love the island. Yet the way of life has changed a great deal since the arrival of the first incomers in the early 1970s. The biggest changes have come about through the introduction of the ro-ro ferry service opening up the two-way communications between the island

and the outside world. This development is seen by the locals as a tremendous boon to the island but, at he same time, it has helped to destroy the very things that attracted some of the incomers in the first place, namely, peace and solitude.

The enhancement of the quality of life brought about by the introduction of a modern ferry service responding to the needs of the island communities it serves has had the desired effect of arresting depopulation, and perhaps even reversing it. It is now possible for Rousay people to commute daily to their work on the Mainland. The main beneficiaries of this flexibility so far are probably the island children who attend secondary school in Kirkwall and who are now able to continue living at home instead of going into hostel accommodation in the town.

It seems to me that the effect the incomers have had on the way of life in Rousay is fairly small considering that they out-number the locals by two to one. The changes which stem from the introduction of the ro-ro ferry are very much more marked. The incomers appear to be a collection of individuals who are not inclined towards united action to achieve their aims. Were they so inclined, the effect of their numbers on the island's way of life would be more marked than it is.

Although Rousay's depopulation has been halted by the arrival of people from the south, I fear that the proportion of the population made up of locals will become even smaller than it is at present. How sad it is that the neighbouring island of Egilsay has only one resident who is a native born Orcadian. Is Rousay heading down that road?

The locals have resignedly accepted the arrival of their new neighbours. When asked for their views most of them reply, 'What sort of state would Rousay be in if these people hadn't come to settle here?' For most, acceptance has grown into a polite but cautious welcome, and in many cases into friendship as the locals and incomers get to know each other and bend a little to one another's ways. Over the years there has been some conflict, not of a lasting nature, which has usually been resolved with the departure of one or two troublesome individuals, and there is now no significant evidence of bad feeling poisoning the island atmosphere.

When the children of the earliest incomers were at school they tended to adopt the local accent as that was what they were hearing from most of their schoolfellows. Now, when the children of locals and incomers are more or less matched in numbers each group is retaining its own accents and speech patterns. Inevitably, some exchange of vocabulary takes place leading to one exasperated local parent finding herself saying to her child, 'It's not a wall; it's a bloody dyke.'

For many generations Orkney dialect words and pronunciations have been gradually disappearing from everyday use. A casual look through Hugh Marwick's *Orkney Norn* or Gregor Lamb's *Orkney Wordbook* will reveal words that were in frequent use 40 or 50 years ago but are now seldom heard. What is happening to children's speech in Rousay will speed up that rate of loss, and the fear is that the process will not even be slowed down, let alone reversed.

When I was a child, anyone heard 'chanting' was mocked and laughed at. For an Orcadian, to chant was to adopt an affected form of speech using English pronunciations, words, and expressions that would not normally be used when talking to a fellow Orcadian. Most Orcadians would draw a distinction between chanting and the occasional need to alter their normal form of speech in order to accommodate those poor unfortunates who cannot understand good Orcadian when they hear hid spokken. Not long ago, I heard a young Orkney father declaring that if he ever heard his son chanting he would skelp his backside.

'How old is your boy?', I asked.

'Six months', he replied.

FULL CIRCLE

Dear Pat,

Here we are, back at the pier where we began our meander around Rousay. On our way I have drawn your attention to some of the main changes that have taken place in the island during my lifetime. Numerous crofts and small farms have been absorbed into a small number of large units so highly mechanised that they give employment to only a tiny fraction of the numbers that were once needed to work the same acreage. The drop in population has been severe with only about 80 native-born Orcadians remaining on the island. This exodus would have been crippling for the island's economy had it not been for the timely arrival of immigrants from the south who bought up properties from the departing locals. Despite this influx of new residents and the variety of skills they have to offer and the introduction of a new industry in the form of fish farming, not enough new jobs have yet been created, in place of those lost on the farms, to support even the present small population of 250.

But there is a brighter side to this picture. The present-day ferries provide a service beyond the dreams of our parents, and have been an important factor, along with the immigration from the south, in reversing, during the past 25 years, the depopulation of the island that was evident for many decades. Along with rising standards of rural housing and the arrival of mains electricity and other services, the improvements in communications have transformed the quality of life in the island. Is it too much to hope that these changes will bring more job opportunities in their wake?

However, it is the things that do not change that bind me to Rousay and keep drawing me back. There is its history, seen in the relics, all over the island, of those strangers who came here down through the millennia and who stayed to till this soil and fish these seas. Every stone of every structure they left behind them has passed through the hands of our forebears. In the ruins of crofthouses and in the kirkyards, memories are revived of folk I knew long ago and of earlier generations known to me only by name but brought close through known ties of kinship.

All these elements are strands of a thread, a continuum of which I feel a part. There are stories that have come down through the ages, and folk-memories of customs of a bygone time, that tell us of a way of life that was largely dictated by the circumstances in which people found themselves and therefore well within our understanding. It is not difficult to see in them earlier versions of ourselves, with the same feelings and failings, the same sense of humour, and the same natural desire, seen in people accustomed to relying on their own resources, to circumvent any petty rules or regulations that get in the way of honest men and commonsense.

There are the memories of childhood and of the pastimes of those innocent years, memories that come flooding back as I revisit former haunts or meet up with old friends. There is the unhurried way of life, mostly heedless of clocks, in which there is time to talk and time to listen, time to think and time to care. All around and always there, is the grandeur of the island scenery, the hills and valleys, the lochs and burns, the fields and dykes and cliffs, the sea and the sky, smiling or frowning according to the vagaries of the weather. Here, as nowhere else I know, I feel at one with my surroundings. It is from the history and the culture and the very fabric of this place that I derive my identity. This is where I belong. This is home

Yours aye,

Robert

ABOUT THE AUTHOR

 Robert C. Marwick was born and brought up on the island of Rousay in Orkney. He received his early education at the Wasbister and Sourin Schools on the island before going on to Kirkwall Grammar School. War service, mainly in the Far East, took up the next five years. He then enrolled at Aberdeen University and after graduation trained to become a teacher. His first teaching post was in Caithness but after two years he moved to Ayrshire where he taught in four successive schools, in three of them as headmaster. At the time of his retiral he was head of a large primary school in Kilwinning, where he now resides.

Also available:

Rousay Roots. Published by the author. First edition 1994. Second edition 1995. Third edition 1999.

From My Rousay Schoolbag. Brinnoven, Livingston. 1995.